Jaida,

I have really enjoyed working with you. I will keep you busy Substituting. if Mike don't Keep you to busy working for him. You are very sweet and I will miss you.

Love,
Angie Vaughn
528-1553
"Call me Sometime"

We will miss you.
When you make a Batch of
Cookies you must bring a
sample. Jannie Worley
12-97

Dear Jaida —
I can never express in
words my gratitude for all
you have done for me. You
have been an extremely dedicated
employee who has done so much
for the faculty and students of our
school. You deserve the best life
has to offer, I have enjoyed sharing
your family as well. Keep in touch,
and if you ever need anything
I can help with, let me know.
Love Connie
McBride

Jaida,
Good luck
to you &
"new job." I
know you are
going to enjoy
having time
to do things

TO: Jaida Campbell
December 1997

you enjoy.
Cathy Jackson

Mrs. Fields

Best Ever Cookie Book!

By Debbi Fields
and the Editors of Time-Life Books

Time-Life Books, Alexandria, Virginia

CONTENTS

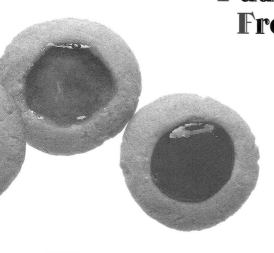

INTRODUCTION

The incomparable Mrs. Debbi Fields has been mixing, baking, and sharing her cookies with America's cookie lovers for more than 20 years. But there's more to Mrs. Fields than cookies: She has also put her stamp on memorable pies, cakes, puddings, candies, and frozen treats.

This new collection of kitchen-tested recipes may become the only dessert cookbook you'll ever need. Along with over 100 recipes to satisfy every possible cookie craving, you will find 100 more that include elegant desserts for a dinner party, easy candies that kids can make, pies for any occasion, and the most luscious cheesecakes imaginable.

You don't have to be an experienced baker to use this book. The recipes are written in an easy-to-follow style. All that you'll need are a kitchen, a few ingredients, and an hour of your time. If you have never baked before, start with drop cookies, or bars, or the well-named Really Easy Chocolate Dessert on page 194. In no time at all, you will be impressing friends and family with a showstopping Lemon Custard Cake *(page 173)* or a Peanut Butter Cream Pie *(page 135)*.

Before you preheat the oven and start creaming the butter and sugar for your first recipe, take a few minutes to look over these four pages; they're packed with tips and hints that will ensure your baking success.

EQUIPMENT

You don't need special equipment to bake anything in this book, but if your cookware is looking worn, here are some suggestions.

MEASURING CUPS For flour, sugar, and other dry ingredients, you should have a set of cups that measure ¼, ⅓, ½, and 1 cup. Metal is better than plastic. Measure liquids in a clear glass calibrated cup with a pour spout.

MIXING BOWLS Whether it's a time-worn crockery bowl or a shiny stainless steel one, it really doesn't matter what type of bowl you use to mix cookies and bars.

It does matter, however, when it comes to beating egg whites for meringues—spotless stainless steel is best because it is the easiest to keep clean. Remember, even a tiny amount of fat on the bowl will prevent the whites from achieving their greatest volume. You might also choose a metal bowl for whipping cream because you can chill it quickly before you use it.

WHISK A wire balloon whisk is the perfect tool for quickly and thoroughly blending the dry ingredients in a recipe.

DOUBLE BOILER While not absolutely necessary, a double boiler takes the worry out of melting chocolate. Just be sure that you are working over hot, but not simmering, water.

COOKIE SHEETS When you buy good-quality, heavy cookie sheets, you're investing in a little baking insurance. Heavier sheets won't warp and develop hot spots, and they let cookies brown more evenly with less chance of burning. The double-layered or cushioned cookie sheets are quite good for baking, too. Have at least two cookie sheets on hand. That way, while one is in the oven, you can be getting the next batch of cookies ready.

BAKING PANS can be made of metal or glass, but cakes and bars bake slightly faster in glass pans. If you don't have the exact pan size or shape called for by a recipe, use a pan whose surface area is close to the one specified. For instance, if the recipe specifies a 7-by-11-inch pan (77-square-inch surface area), a 9-by-9-inch pan (81 square inches) is a fine substitute. If you do opt for a larger pan, shorten the baking time.

PARCHMENT PAPER Also known as baker's parchment, parchment paper is available in large sheets or rolls. You can use it to line cookie sheets and cake pans to prevent sticking. While less expensive wax paper will often do instead, parchment is essential for cookies that tend to stick, such as meringues. You can find parchment paper at kitchen shops and large supermarkets.

PASTRY BAG & STAR TIP While you might want a pastry bag and star tip to decorate some of the fancy cakes and pastries found in Chapter 5, it's not a requirement. You could just as easily use a narrow spatula to create decorative swirls on top of Fudgy Studded Buttercream Cake *(page 165)*. Pastry bags are also good for filling tartlet shells, as in the Creamy Chocolate Fantasy *(page 142)*. A large zippered plastic bag makes a handy substitute for a pastry bag: Spoon the filling into the bag, zip shut, and snip a hole in one corner.

INGREDIENTS

When it comes to making these recipes, use the best ingredients you can find. You can locate the ingredients for any recipe in the book at a well-stocked supermarket. When you make out your grocery list, be sure to read the ingredient list carefully and jot down even the minor details. You don't want to find yourself at the store wondering if it was unsweetened or semisweet chocolate that goes into the Chocolate Raspberry Rhapsody *(page 174)*.

Only butter will give a true buttery flavor to your baking. Margarine will certainly work in these recipes, but the desserts just won't taste as good. Do not substitute shortening for butter. Read carefully to see if the recipe you are about to make calls for salted or unsalted butter. If it calls for 2 sticks salted butter and you have only unsalted, add ¾ teaspoon salt to the dry ingredients. If it calls for unsalted butter, and you have the salted version, omit any other salt in the recipe. The best way to soften butter is to leave it out on the countertop for at least an hour. The most enjoyable way to soften it is to place the butter between two sheets of plastic wrap and bash it with a heavy mallet or rolling pin. You can also soften butter in the microwave oven, but be very careful: heat it for only a few seconds at medium-low power or it will melt.

The recipes have all been tested with large eggs.

Most of the desserts in this book are made with all-purpose white flour. From time to time, you'll find recipes, such as the luscious Lemon Custard Cake *(page 173)* or the Ganache-Filled Devil's Food Cake *(page 167)*, call for cake flour, which is a finely ground, soft white flour. Cake flour produces a tender, delectable crumb. If you don't have cake flour, replace 2 tablespoons of flour with cornstarch for each cup of all-purpose white flour. Sift before adding to your batter. On occasion, the recipes combine whole-wheat flour with white flour to add a chewier quality to the dough. The Peanut Butter Oatmeal Ranch Cookies *(page 25)* and the Pineapple Pocket Pies *(page 65)* take advantage of the added flavor.

For the fullest vanilla flavor, choose top-quality vanilla extract, never an imitation vanilla.

Nuts add rich flavor and a satisfying chewiness to baked goods. Be aware that they contain a fair amount of natural oils and will become rancid if stored too long at room temperature. Store shelled nuts in an airtight container in the freezer. To enhance their nutty flavor, toast nuts before adding to a recipe. To toast walnuts, pecans, almonds, hazelnuts, or macadamia nuts, spread them in a single layer in a metal baking pan. Toast in a 325°F oven, shaking the pan once or twice, until the nuts are fragrant and very lightly colored, about 5 minutes. Quickly transfer them to a plate and let cool. You can also toast nuts in a skillet on top of the stove, but they are more likely to burn with skillet toasting.

Two-thirds of the recipes in this book call for chocolate in one form or another. As you bake more and more of these desserts, you'll become familiar with the many types of chocolate available to cooks. The Chocolate Carmalua *(page 158),* for instance, depends on unsweetened and bittersweet chocolate to give an intense richness to the cake, while semisweet chocolate mellows its chocolate-caramel glaze. Quality is crucial when it comes to chocolate: Choose a brand you enjoy eating out of hand. Beware of chocolate chips that are very inexpensive, as low price is a good indicator of poor quality. Never use an imitation chocolate.

GETTING AHEAD

Here are a few time-saving tips:

● Mix up batches of cookie dough in advance. Form the cookies on a cookie sheet and freeze until solid. Then remove the frozen cookies and pop them into a plastic bag, sealing tightly. Keep them frozen until you're ready to bake. You don't need to thaw the dough before baking.

● Consider making bar cookies instead of fancier cookies. There's no forming or rolling or cutting, and the dough is baked all at once. You can bake bars in an aluminum-foil pan; cool, then freeze the bars, pan and all. Alternatively, line a baking pan with enough foil to come up well beyond its sides before filling and baking. When cool, lift out the entire uncut layer, wrap, and freeze.

● Chocolate freezes well. When making a chocolate layer cake, double the cake recipe and freeze extra layers. That way, if you need a cake in a hurry, you can just thaw the layers and frost them.

● If you intend to bring a warm quick bread or muffins into the office for a morning meeting, organize everything the night before. Measure and blend the dry ingredients. Take the butter out of the refrigerator to soften. Have all other ingredients lined up and ready to go. That way, it takes only 10 minutes to mix everything in the early a.m.

STORAGE

Storage may not concern you, particularly if you bake when hungry family members are within range, but on occasion you might have some treats that you want to keep out of reach.

Airtight is the key word when it comes to storing cookies. They will stay chewier and won't absorb unwanted aromas or flavors if packed into an airtight

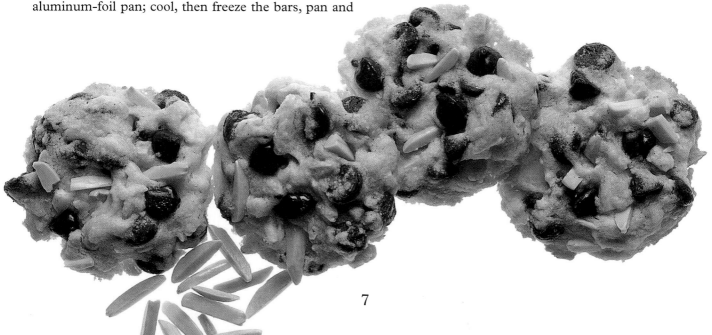

plastic container or cookie tin. Also, cookies, brownies, and bars will be good for up to six months in the freezer, as long as they are sealed in plastic bags.

Cover pies and cakes with plastic wrap and store them in the refrigerator. Use a few strategically placed toothpicks to keep the plastic from disturbing the surface of a decorated cake. For fullest flavor, bring them back to room temperature before serving. Obviously, ice cream desserts should be stored well wrapped in the freezer. Do take them out a few minutes before serving

to bring out the full flavor of the ice cream.

Store chocolate candies in the refrigerator to keep them from melting. It's also a good idea to refrigerate desserts frosted with chocolate ganache—a mixture of chocolate, butter, and cream—until 30 minutes before serving.

Some soft baked goods—Debbi's Deadly Chocolate Muffins *(page 180)* or the Low-Fat Chocolate Cookies *(page 33)*—become gummy if wrapped airtight. These are best eaten within a day or two of baking. Otherwise, freeze for longer storage.

8

Drop Cookies

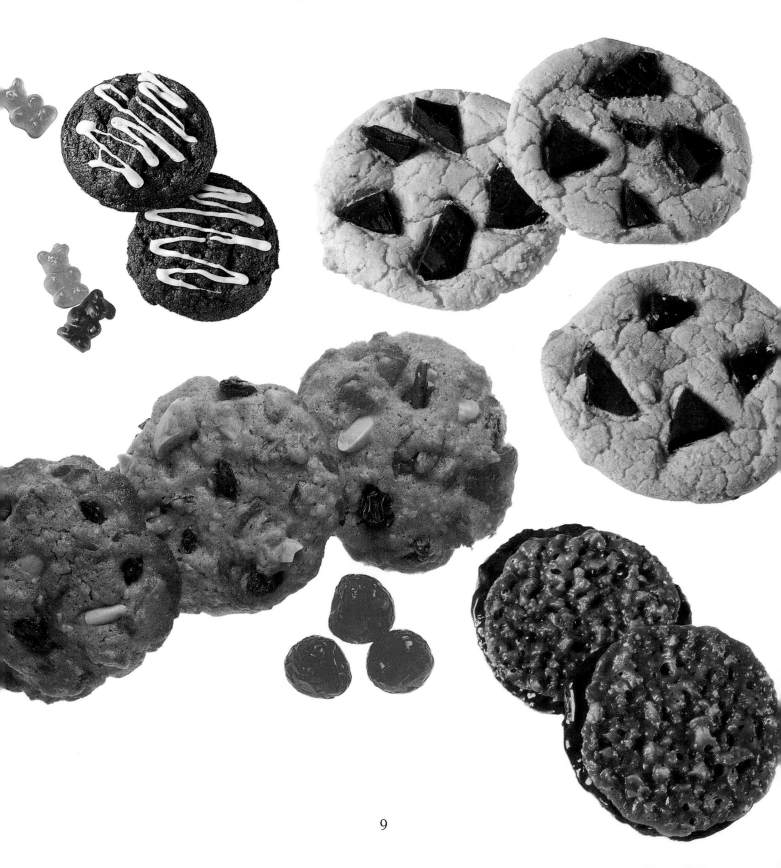

Choc-Co-Chunks

2¼ cups all-purpose flour
1 teaspoon baking soda
1½ sticks (¾ cup) unsalted butter, softened
1 cup (packed) dark brown sugar
2 large eggs
2 teaspoons vanilla extract

1⅓ cups shredded coconut
12 ounces white chocolate, cut into chunks
1 cup coarsely chopped macadamia nuts

Yield: About 3 dozen

- Preheat the oven to 300°F.

- In a small bowl, combine the flour and baking soda.

- In a medium bowl with an electric mixer, cream the butter and sugar. Beat in the eggs and vanilla. Beat in the flour mixture; do not overmix. Stir in the coconut, white chocolate chunks, and macadamia nuts.

- Drop the dough by rounded tablespoons 2 inches apart onto an ungreased cookie sheet. Bake for 18 to 20 minutes. Transfer to a wire rack to cool.

Blue-Ribbon Chocolate Chip Cookies

2½ cups all-purpose flour
½ teaspoon baking soda
¼ teaspoon salt
1 cup (packed) dark brown sugar
½ cup granulated sugar
2 sticks (1 cup) salted butter, softened

2 large eggs
2 teaspoons vanilla extract
12 ounces semisweet chocolate chips
   (about 2 cups)

Yield: About 3½ dozen

- Preheat oven to 300°F.

- In medium bowl, combine flour, soda, and salt. Mix well with wire whisk. Set aside.

- In a large bowl with an electric mixer, blend sugars at medium speed. Add butter and mix to form a grainy paste, scraping down the sides of the bowl. Add eggs and vanilla extract, and mix at medium speed until just blended. Do not overmix.

- Add the flour mixture and chocolate chips, and blend at low speed until just barely mixed. Do not overmix.

- Drop the dough by rounded tablespoons onto an ungreased cookie sheet, 2 inches apart. Bake for 18 to 22 minutes or until golden brown. Transfer cookies immediately to a cool surface with a spatula.

Drop each heaping tablespoon of dough onto the cookie sheet, taking care to leave about 2 inches between each cookie. As they bake, the cookies will spread.

Apple Oatmeal Cookies

COOKIES
2½ cups all-purpose flour
1 cup quick oats (not instant)
½ teaspoon salt
1 teaspoon baking soda
1 teaspoon ground cinnamon
¼ teaspoon ground cloves
2 teaspoons grated lemon zest
  (1 medium lemon)
1 cup (packed) dark brown sugar
1½ sticks (¾ cup) salted butter, softened

1 large egg
½ cup unsweetened applesauce
½ cup honey
1 cup fresh apple, peeled and finely chopped
  (1 medium apple)
6 ounces raisins (about 1 cup)

TOPPING
½ cup quick oats (not instant)

Yield: About 4 dozen

- Preheat oven to 300°F.

- In medium bowl combine flour, oats, salt, soda, cinnamon, cloves, and lemon zest. Mix well with a wire whisk. Set aside.

- Cream sugar and butter together in a large bowl using an electric mixer. Add egg, applesauce, and honey and beat at medium speed until smooth.

- Add the flour mixture, fresh apple, and raisins, and blend at low speed until just combined. Do not overmix. Dough will be quite soft.

- Drop by rounded tablespoons onto ungreased cookie sheets, 1½ inches apart. If you wish, sprinkle the cookies with oats. Bake for 18 to 22 minutes or until bottoms are golden.

Pumpkin Harvest Cookies

2¼ cups all-purpose flour
1 teaspoon pumpkin pie spice
½ teaspoon baking soda
2 sticks (1 cup) unsalted butter
1½ cups (packed) dark brown sugar
1 cup solid-packed unsweetened pumpkin
  purée

2 large eggs
1 tablespoon vanilla extract
10 ounces white chocolate, coarsely chopped
1 cup pecan halves and pieces, toasted

Yield: About 3 dozen

- Preheat the oven to 300°F.

- In a small bowl, combine the flour, pumpkin pie spice, and baking soda.

- In a medium bowl with an electric mixer, cream the butter and sugar. Beat in the pumpkin purée. Beat in the eggs and vanilla. Beat in the flour mixture until just combined. Stir in the white chocolate and pecans.

- Drop the dough by rounded tablespoons 2 inches apart onto an ungreased cookie sheet. Bake for 20 to 22 minutes, or until just set. Transfer to wire racks to cool.

13

Chocolate Chip Dough to Go

2 cups all-purpose flour
1 cup quick oats (not instant)
½ teaspoon baking powder
¼ teaspoon salt
2 sticks (1 cup) unsalted butter, softened
¾ cup (packed) light brown sugar
¾ cup granulated sugar

2 large eggs
2 teaspoons vanilla extract
1 cup coarsely chopped pecans
12 ounces semisweet chocolate chips
  (about 2 cups)

Yield: About 4 dozen

- In a medium bowl, combine the flour, oats, baking powder, and salt. In another medium bowl with an electric mixer, cream the butter and sugars. Beat in the eggs and vanilla. Gently beat in the flour mixture; then stir in the pecans and chocolate chips.

- Turn half of the dough out onto a sheet of wax paper. Shape into a log 2 inches in diameter. Roll up the log of dough in the wax paper and twist the ends closed. Repeat with the remaining dough.

Chill until firm. The cookie dough can be refrigerated for 1 week or frozen for 6 months stored in an airtight plastic bag.

- To bake the cookies, preheat the oven to 300°F. If using frozen dough, let it soften slightly at room temperature, then cut the dough log into ½-inch-thick slices. Place the slices on an ungreased cookie sheet 2 inches apart. Bake for 22 to 24 minutes, or until set.

Cut the chilled dough into ½-inch-thick slices and place 2 inches apart on an ungreased cookie sheet.

Malted Milk Cookies

2½ cups all-purpose flour
¾ cup plain malted milk powder
½ teaspoon baking soda
¼ teaspoon salt
1 cup granulated sugar
½ cup (packed) light brown sugar
2 sticks (1 cup) salted butter, softened

2 large eggs
2 teaspoons vanilla extract
2 tablespoons sweetened condensed milk
12 ounces milk chocolate chips
  (about 2 cups)

Yield: About 3½ dozen

- Preheat oven to 300°F.

- In medium bowl, combine flour, malted milk powder, soda, and salt. Mix well with a wire whisk. Set aside.

- Blend sugars using an electric mixer set at medium speed. Add butter and mix, occasionally scraping down the sides of the bowl. Add the eggs, vanilla, and condensed milk, and beat at medium speed until light and fluffy.

- Add the flour mixture and chocolate chips, and blend at low speed until just combined. Do not overmix.

- Drop by rounded tablespoons onto ungreased cookie sheets, 2 inches apart. Bake for 22 to 25 minutes until cookies are slightly brown along edges. Transfer cookies immediately to cool surface with a spatula.

Carrot Fruit Jumbles

2½ cups all-purpose flour
1 teaspoon baking soda
½ teaspoon baking powder
½ teaspoon ground cloves
2 teaspoons ground cinnamon
¼ teaspoon salt
1 cup quick oats (not instant)
¾ cup (packed) dark brown sugar
¾ cup granulated sugar

2 sticks (1 cup) salted butter, softened
2 large eggs
2 teaspoons vanilla extract
2 cups grated carrot
  (2 or 3 medium carrots)
½ cup crushed pineapple, drained
4 ounces chopped walnuts (about 1 cup)

Yield: About 4 dozen

- Preheat oven to 350°F.

- In a medium bowl combine flour, soda, baking powder, cloves, cinnamon, salt, and oats. Mix well with a wire whisk and set aside.

- In a large bowl with an electric mixer, blend sugars. Add butter and mix to form a grainy paste. Scrape down the sides of bowl.

- Add eggs and vanilla, and beat at medium speed until light and fluffy. Add carrots, pineapple, and nuts, and blend until combined. Batter will appear lumpy.

- Add flour mixture and blend at low speed until just combined. Do not overmix.

- Drop by rounded teaspoons onto ungreased cookie sheets, 1½ inches apart. Bake for 13 to 15 minutes, taking care not to brown cookies. Immediately transfer cookies with a spatula to a cool, flat surface.

Kids Bake 'Em Cookies

1¼ cups all-purpose flour
½ teaspoon baking soda
⅛ teaspoon salt
1 stick (½ cup) salted butter, softened
¼ cup granulated sugar

½ cup honey
6 ounces semisweet chocolate chips
  (about 1 cup)

Yield: About 2 dozen

- Preheat oven 300°F.

- In a small bowl combine flour, soda, and salt. Mix well with a wire whisk and set aside.

- In a medium bowl, blend butter, sugar, and honey with an electric mixer at medium speed. Beat until light and soft, then scrape sides of bowl.

- Add the flour mixture and chocolate chips, and blend at low speed just until combined. Do not overmix.

- Drop dough by rounded teaspoons onto ungreased cookie sheets, 1½ inches apart. Bake for 18 to 20 minutes or until light golden brown. Immediately transfer cookies with a spatula to a cool, flat surface.

Pecan Supremes

2 cups all-purpose flour
½ teaspoon baking soda
¼ teaspoon salt
¾ cup quick oats (not instant)
¾ cup (packed) dark brown sugar
¾ cup granulated sugar
2 sticks (1 cup) salted butter, softened

2 large eggs
2 teaspoons vanilla extract
4 ounces chopped pecans (about 1 cup)
6 ounces semisweet chocolate chips
   (about 1 cup)

Yield: About 3 dozen

- Preheat oven to 300°F.

- In a medium bowl combine flour, soda, salt, and oats. Mix well with wire whisk and set aside.

- In a large bowl, blend sugars with an electric mixer at medium speed. Add butter and mix to form a grainy paste. Scrape down sides of bowl, then add eggs and vanilla. Beat at medium speed until light and fluffy.

- Add the flour mixture, pecans, and chocolate chips, and blend at low speed just until combined. Do not overmix.

- Drop dough by rounded tablespoons onto ungreased cookie sheets, 1½ inches apart. Bake for 18 to 20 minutes. Immediately transfer cookies with a spatula to a cool, flat surface.

Double-Chocolate Peanut Butter Cookies

6 ounces semisweet chocolate, coarsely
  chopped
2 cups all-purpose flour
½ teaspoon baking soda
¼ teaspoon salt
¾ cup (packed) dark brown sugar
¾ cup granulated sugar
2 sticks (1 cup) unsalted butter, softened

1 cup creamy peanut butter
2 large eggs
2 teaspoons vanilla extract
12 ounces milk chocolate chips
  (about 2 cups)
24 to 30 whole shelled peanuts

Yield: About 2 dozen

- Preheat the oven to 300°F. In a double boiler, melt the semisweet chocolate over hot, not simmering, water. Set aside to cool to about room temperature.

- In a small bowl, combine the flour, baking soda, and salt.

- In a medium bowl, combine the brown and granulated sugars, then add the butter and beat until well combined. Add the peanut butter and beat until smooth. Add the eggs and vanilla, and beat until just combined. Add the flour mixture and the milk chocolate chips, and beat until no streaks of flour are visible.

- Pour in the melted chocolate and mix partially with a wooden spoon until marbleized. Drop the dough in 3-tablespoon mounds 2 inches apart onto an ungreased cookie sheet. Top each with one whole peanut. Bake for 23 minutes, or until just set but still soft. Cool on the cookie sheet for 30 seconds, then transfer to wire racks to cool completely.

Near right, beat the peanut butter into the butter-sugar mixture. Far right, before baking, press a whole peanut into the center of each mound of cookie dough.

White Chocolate Cookies with Chocolate Chunks

· · · · · · · · · · · · · · · ·

2 sticks (1 cup) unsalted butter, softened
2½ cups all-purpose flour
1 teaspoon baking soda
¼ teaspoon salt
3 ounces white chocolate, finely chopped
½ cup granulated sugar

½ cup (packed) light brown sugar
2 large eggs, at room temperature
2 teaspoons vanilla extract
8 ounces semisweet chocolate, cut into chunks

Yield: About 3 dozen

- Preheat the oven to 300°F. Cut 4 tablespoons of the butter into ¼-inch cubes.

- In a small bowl, combine the flour, baking soda, and salt.

- In a double boiler, melt the white chocolate with the butter, stirring until melted and smooth, about 10 minutes. Set aside to cool slightly.

- In a large bowl with an electric mixer, cream the remaining 1½ sticks of butter with the granulated and brown sugars. Beat in the eggs one at a time,

beating well after each addition. Beat in the white chocolate mixture and vanilla. On low speed, gradually beat in the flour mixture until just combined. Stir in the semisweet chocolate chunks.

- Drop the dough by rounded tablespoons 2 inches apart onto an ungreased cookie sheet. Bake for about 20 minutes, or until the edges of the cookies begin to brown lightly (the cookies will still be soft in the center). Cool on the cookie sheet for 1 minute, then transfer to wire racks to cool completely.

Mocha Chunk Cookies

2½ cups all-purpose flour
⅓ cup unsweetened cocoa powder
½ teaspoon baking soda
¼ teaspoon salt
2 teaspoons instant coffee crystals
    (French roast or other dark coffee)
2 teaspoons coffee liqueur
1 cup granulated sugar

¾ cup (packed) dark brown sugar
2 sticks (1 cup) salted butter, softened
2 large eggs
10 ounces semisweet chocolate bar,
    coarsely chopped (about 2 cups)

Yield: About 4 dozen

- Preheat oven to 300°F.

- In a medium bowl, combine flour, cocoa, soda, and salt. Mix well with a wire whisk and set aside.

- In a small bowl, dissolve coffee crystals in coffee liqueur and set aside.

- In a large bowl, blend sugars with an electric mixer at medium speed. Add butter and mix to form a grainy paste. Scrape down sides of bowl. Then add eggs and dissolved coffee crystals, and beat at medium speed until smooth.

- Add the flour mixture and chocolate chunks, and blend at low speed just until combined. Do not overmix.

- Drop by rounded tablespoons onto ungreased cookie sheet, 2 inches apart. Bake for 20 to 22 minutes. Immediately transfer cookies with a spatula to a cool, flat surface.

Banana Nut Cookies

2⅔ cups all-purpose flour
½ teaspoon baking soda
¼ teaspoon salt
1 cup (packed) light brown sugar
½ cup granulated sugar
2 sticks (1 cup) salted butter, softened
1 large egg
1 teaspoon crème de bananes liqueur or

banana extract
¾ cup mashed ripe banana
  (1 medium banana)
12 ounces semisweet chocolate chips
  (about 2 cups)
4 ounces chopped walnuts (about 1 cup)

Yield: About 4 dozen

- Preheat oven to 300°F.

- In medium bowl, combine flour, soda, and salt. Mix well with a wire whisk. Set aside.

- In large bowl with an electric mixer blend sugars at medium speed. Add butter and mix to form a grainy paste, scraping down the sides of the bowl. Add egg, liqueur, and banana, and beat at medium speed until smooth.

- Add the flour mixture, 1 cup of the chocolate chips, and the walnuts, and blend at low speed until just combined. Do not overmix.

- Drop by rounded tablespoons onto ungreased cookie sheets, 2 inches apart. Sprinkle cookies with chocolate chips, 6 to 8 per cookie. Bake for 20 to 24 minutes or until cookie edges begin to brown. Transfer immediately to a cool surface with a spatula.

Chocolate Mint Cookies

2⅔ cups all-purpose flour
½ teaspoon baking soda
¼ teaspoon salt
½ cup unsweetened cocoa powder
¾ cup (packed) light brown sugar
⅔ cup granulated sugar
2 sticks (1 cup) salted butter, softened

3 large eggs
1 teaspoon mint extract
10 ounces mint chocolate chips
  (about 1¾ cups)

Yield: About 3 dozen

- Preheat oven to 300°F.

- In a medium bowl, combine flour, soda, salt, and cocoa powder. Mix well with a wire whisk and set aside.

- In a large bowl, blend sugars with an electric mixer at medium speed. Add butter and beat to form a grainy paste. Scrape sides of bowl, then add eggs and mint extract. Beat at medium speed until light and fluffy.

- Add the flour mixture and chocolate chips, and blend at low speed just until combined. Do not overmix.

- Drop dough by rounded tablespoons onto ungreased cookie sheets, 1½ inches apart. Bake for 19 to 21 minutes. Immediately transfer cookies with a spatula to a cool, flat surface.

Lemon Chocolate Chip Buttons

2 cups all-purpose flour
½ teaspoon baking soda
1 teaspoon ground coriander
1½ sticks (¾ cup) salted butter, softened
1 cup granulated sugar
2 large eggs

1½ teaspoons lemon extract
9 ounces mini chocolate chips
  (about 1½ cups)

Yield: About 4 dozen

- Preheat oven to 300°F.

- In a medium bowl combine flour, soda, and coriander with a wire whisk. Set aside.

- In a large bowl cream butter and sugar with an electric mixer at medium speed to form a grainy paste. Add eggs and lemon extract, and beat well. Scrape down sides of bowl.

- Add the flour mixture and the chocolate chips, and blend at low speed just until combined. Do not overmix.

- Drop dough by teaspoons onto ungreased cookie sheets, 1½ inches apart. Bake for 14 to 15 minutes on center rack of oven. Do not brown. Immediately transfer cookies with a spatula to a cool, flat surface.

Peanut Butter Oatmeal Ranch Cookies

¾ cup whole-wheat flour
¾ cup all-purpose flour
½ teaspoon baking powder
1 cup oats (old fashioned or quick)
1 cup (packed) light brown sugar
1 stick (½ cup) salted butter, softened
½ cup creamy peanut butter

¼ cup honey
2 large eggs
2 teaspoons vanilla extract
6 ounces raisins (about 1 cup)
3 ounces sunflower seeds (about ½ cup)

Yield: About 3 dozen

- Preheat oven to 300°F.

- In a medium bowl, combine flours, baking powder, and oats. Mix well with a wire whisk and set aside.

- In a large bowl, beat sugar and butter with an electric mixer at medium speed to form a grainy paste. Blend together the peanut butter, honey, eggs, and vanilla. Scrape down sides of bowl.

- Add the flour mixture, raisins, and sunflower seeds. Blend at low speed just until combined. Do not overmix.

- Drop by rounded tablespoons onto ungreased cookie sheets, 2 inches apart. Bake for 18 to 22 minutes until bottoms turn golden brown. Immediately transfer cookies with a spatula to a cool, flat surface.

Cashew and Coconut Cookies

2¼ cups all-purpose flour
½ teaspoon baking soda
¼ teaspoon salt
¾ cup (packed) light brown sugar
½ cup granulated sugar
1½ sticks (¾ cup) salted butter, softened
2 large eggs
2 teaspoons vanilla extract

½ cup sweetened shredded coconut
4 ounces chopped, unsalted raw
  cashews (about 1 cup)
4 ounces chopped dates (about 1 cup)
2 ounces sweetened shredded coconut
  (about ¼ cup), reserved for topping

Yield: About 2½ dozen

- Preheat oven to 300°F.

- In a medium bowl, combine flour, soda, and salt. Mix well with a wire whisk and set aside.

- In a medium bowl, combine sugars with an electric mixer at medium speed. Add butter and mix to form a grainy paste. Add eggs and vanilla, and beat until smooth.

- Add flour mixture, coconut, cashews, and dates. Blend at low speed just until combined. Do not overmix.

Sprinkle about a teaspoon of coconut on top of each cookie before sliding the sheets into the oven. When the cookies have finished baking, the coconut will take on a golden, toasted color.

- Drop by rounded tablespoons onto ungreased cookie sheets, 2 inches apart. Sprinkle tops lightly with reserved coconut.

- Bake for 18 to 22 minutes or until bottoms turn golden brown. With a spatula, transfer cookies to a cool, flat surface.

Fruitcake Cookies

2 cups all-purpose flour
½ teaspoon baking powder
1 cup quick oats (not instant)
2 sticks (1 cup) salted butter, softened
1½ cups (packed) light brown sugar
¼ cup unsulfurized molasses
2 teaspoons brandy
2 teaspoons vanilla extract
2 teaspoons almond extract

2 large eggs
3 ounces raisins (about ½ cup)
4 ounces chopped pecans (about 1 cup)
2 ounces chopped almonds (about ½ cup)
13½ ounces candied cherries, chopped
  (about 2 cups)

Yield: About 4½ dozen

• Preheat oven to 300°F.

• In a medium bowl, combine flour, baking powder, and oats. Mix well with a wire whisk and set aside.

• In a large bowl, cream butter and sugar with an electric mixer at medium speed. Mix to form a grainy paste. Add molasses, brandy, almond and vanilla extracts and eggs; beat until smooth.

• Add flour mixture, raisins, pecans, almonds, and cherries. Blend at low speed just until combined. Do not overmix.

• Drop by rounded tablespoons onto ungreased cookie sheets, 1½ inches apart. Bake for 22 to 24 minutes or until cookies are set.

• Let cookies set on sheets for a few minutes, then transfer to a cool, flat surface. Top each cookie with a candied cherry half.

These cookies are fruitcake made easy. You just blend everything in your mixer—first the dry ingredients, then the wet, and finally the fruit pieces. Both a hand mixer or a stand-up mixer work fine.

Chocolate Chip Raisin Cookies

2 cups all-purpose flour
½ teaspoon baking powder
⅓ cup (packed) light brown sugar
1 cup granulated sugar
2 sticks (1 cup) salted butter, softened
2 large eggs

2 teaspoons vanilla extract
12 ounces raisins (about 2 cups)
12 ounces semisweet chocolate chips
  (about 2 cups)

Yield: About 4½ dozen

- Preheat oven to 300°F.

- In medium bowl, combine flour and baking powder. Mix well with wire whisk. Set aside.

- Blend sugars in a large bowl using an electric mixer set at medium speed. Add butter and mix until grainy, scraping down the sides of the bowl. Add eggs and vanilla extract, and mix at medium speed until smooth.

- Add the flour mixture, raisins, and chocolate chips. Blend at low speed until just combined. Do not overmix.

- Drop by rounded tablespoons onto ungreased cookie sheets, 1½ inches apart. Bake for 18 to 20 minutes. Transfer cookies immediately to a cool, flat surface using a spatula.

Orange Chocolate Chunk Cookies

2½ cups all-purpose flour
½ teaspoon baking soda
¼ teaspoon salt
1 teaspoon grated orange peel
  (1 medium orange)
1 cup granulated sugar
½ cup (packed) light brown sugar

2 sticks (1 cup) salted butter, softened
2 large eggs
1 teaspoon orange extract
8 ounces semisweet chocolate bar, coarsely
  chopped (about 1½ cups)

Yield: About 2½ dozen

- Preheat oven to 300°F.

- In a medium bowl, combine flour, soda, salt, and orange peel. Mix well with a wire whisk and set aside.

- In a large bowl, blend sugars with an electric mixer at medium speed. Add butter and beat to form a grainy paste, scraping sides of bowl if needed. Add eggs and orange extract, and beat at medium speed until light and fluffy.

- Add the flour mixture and chopped chocolate. Blend at low speed just until combined. Do not overmix.

- Drop by rounded tablespoons onto ungreased cookie sheets, 1½ inches apart. Bake for 18 to 22 minutes until cookies are slightly brown along edges. Transfer cookies immediately to a cool surface with a spatula.

Eggnog Cookies

2¼ cups all-purpose flour
1 teaspoon baking powder
½ teaspoon ground cinnamon
½ teaspoon ground nutmeg
1¼ cups granulated sugar
1½ sticks (¾ cup) salted butter, softened

½ cup eggnog
1 teaspoon vanilla extract
2 large egg yolks
1 tablespoon ground nutmeg

Yield: About 3 dozen

- Preheat oven to 300°F.

- In a medium bowl, combine flour, baking powder, cinnamon, and nutmeg. Mix well with a wire whisk and set aside.

- In a large bowl, cream sugar and butter with an electric mixer to form a grainy paste. Add eggnog, vanilla, and egg yolks and beat at medium speed until smooth.

- Add the flour mixture and beat at low speed just until combined. Do not overmix.

- Drop by rounded teaspoons onto ungreased cookie sheets, 1 inch apart. Sprinkle lightly with nutmeg. Bake for 23 to 25 minutes or until bottoms turn light brown. Transfer to cool, flat surface immediately with a spatula.

Black-and-Whites

2¼ cups all-purpose flour
½ cup unsweetened cocoa powder
½ teaspoon baking soda
¼ teaspoon salt
1 cup (packed) dark brown sugar
¾ cup granulated sugar
2 sticks (1 cup) salted butter, softened
3 large eggs

2 teaspoons vanilla extract
5¼ ounces semisweet chocolate bar, coarsely
  chopped (about 1 cup)
5¼ ounces white chocolate bar, coarsely
  chopped (about 1 cup)

Yield: About 3 dozen

- Preheat oven to 300°F.

- In medium bowl, combine flour, cocoa, soda, and salt. Mix well with a wire whisk. Set aside.

- Blend sugars in a large bowl using an electric mixer set at medium speed. Add butter and mix to form a grainy paste, scraping down the sides of the bowl. Add eggs and vanilla, and beat at medium speed until smooth.

- Add the flour mixture and chocolates, and blend at low speed until just combined. Do not overmix.

- Drop by rounded tablespoons onto ungreased cookie sheets, 2 inches apart. Bake for 18 to 22 minutes. Transfer cookies immediately to a cool, flat surface.

31

Marbles

2 cups all-purpose flour
½ teaspoon baking powder
¼ teaspoon salt
½ cup (packed) light brown sugar
½ cup granulated sugar
1 stick (½ cup) salted butter, softened
1 large egg

4 ounces sour cream (½ cup)
1 teaspoon vanilla extract
6 ounces semisweet chocolate chips
  (about 1 cup)

Yield: About 2½ dozen

- Preheat oven to 300°F.

- In medium bowl, combine flour, baking powder, and salt with wire whisk. Set aside.

- Combine sugars in a large bowl using an electric mixer set at medium speed. Add butter and beat until batter is grainy. Add egg, sour cream, and vanilla, and beat at medium speed until light and fluffy. Scrape bowl. Add the flour mixture and blend at low speed until just combined. Do not overmix.

- Place chocolate chips in double boiler over hot, but not boiling, water. Stir constantly until melted. Or, place chips in a microwave-proof bowl and microwave on high, stirring every 20 seconds until melted.

- Cool chocolate for a few minutes and pour over cookie batter. Using a wooden spoon or rubber spatula, lightly fold melted chocolate into the dough. Do not mix chocolate completely into cookie dough.

- Drop by rounded tablespoons, 2 inches apart, onto ungreased cookie sheets. Bake for 20 to 22 minutes. Do not brown. Quickly transfer cookies to a cool surface.

Fold the cool melted chocolate into the cookie batter, stirring lightly with a wooden spoon (far left). Continue stirring only until the chocolate is well distributed and creates a swirled, marbleized pattern (left).

Low-Fat Chocolate Cookies

2⅔ cups all-purpose flour
½ cup unsweetened cocoa powder
1 teaspoon baking soda
½ teaspoon salt
¾ cup (packed) dark brown sugar
¾ cup granulated sugar
⅓ cup canola oil

½ cup unsweetened applesauce
3 egg whites
2 teaspoons vanilla extract
½ cup mini semisweet chocolate chips

Yield: About 5½ dozen

- In a medium bowl, combine the flour, cocoa, baking soda, and salt.

- In another medium bowl with an electric mixer, blend the brown and granulated sugars. Slowly beat in the oil. Beat in the applesauce, egg whites, and vanilla, and blend on low speed until smooth.

- Add the flour mixture and blend on low speed until the dough is just combined. Refrigerate the dough until firm, about 1 hour.

- Preheat the oven to 300°F.

- Roll the dough into small 1-inch balls, place on a cookie sheet and flatten slightly. Sprinkle with the mini chocolate chips, then bake for 17 to 19 minutes (do not overbake; when the cookies cool they will get hard). Transfer the cookies to wire racks to cool.

Chocolate Cashew Crunch

½ stick (¼ cup) unsalted butter
⅓ cup (packed) light brown sugar
¼ cup light corn syrup
½ cup finely chopped salted cashews
⅓ cup all-purpose flour

1½ teaspoons vanilla extract
6 ounces milk chocolate chips
  (about 1 cup)

Yield: About 3 dozen

- Preheat the oven to 350°F. Butter and flour a cookie sheet.

- In a small saucepan, melt the butter over medium heat. Add the brown sugar and corn syrup, then bring to a boil over medium heat, stirring constantly, until the sugar dissolves, 3 to 5 minutes. Remove from the heat.

- Stir in the cashews, flour, and vanilla. Drop the batter in ½-teaspoon mounds 2 inches apart onto the prepared cookie sheet. Using a small spatula, spread each mound into a circle.

- Bake for 8 to 10 minutes, or until browned, rotating the pan back to front after 4 minutes. Cool on the cookie sheet for about 30 seconds, then transfer to wire racks to cool completely.

- In a small bowl set over a small saucepan, melt the chocolate over hot, not simmering, water. Dip the cookies halfway into the chocolate and return to the racks to set.

Double-Rich Chocolate Cookies

2½ cups all-purpose flour
½ teaspoon baking soda
¼ teaspoon salt
½ cup unsweetened cocoa powder
1 cup (packed) dark brown sugar
¾ cup granulated sugar
2 sticks (1 cup) salted butter, softened

3 large eggs
2 teaspoons vanilla extract
12 ounces semisweet chocolate chips
  (about 2 cups)

Yield: About 4 dozen

- Preheat oven to 300°F.

- In a medium bowl, combine flour, soda, salt, and cocoa powder. Mix well with a wire whisk and set aside.

- In a large bowl, blend sugars with an electric mixer at medium speed. Add butter and beat to form a grainy paste. Scrape down sides of bowl, then add eggs and vanilla. Beat at medium speed until light and fluffy.

- Add the flour mixture and chocolate chips, and blend at low speed just until combined. Do not overmix.

- Drop dough by rounded tablespoons onto ungreased cookie sheets, 1½ inches apart. Bake for 18 to 22 minutes. Immediately transfer cookies with a spatula to a cool, flat surface.

Mandarin and Marmalade Cookies

2¾ cups all-purpose flour
1 teaspoon baking powder
2 sticks (1 cup) salted butter, softened
1 cup granulated sugar
1 large egg

½ cup orange marmalade
One 10-ounce can mandarin oranges, drained
  and chopped

Yield: About 3½ dozen

- Preheat oven to 300°F.

- In a medium bowl, combine flour and baking powder. Mix well with a wire whisk and set aside.

- In a large bowl, blend butter and sugar with an electric mixer to form a grainy paste. Add egg and orange marmalade, and beat at medium speed until smooth. Add the flour mixture and the oranges, and blend at low speed just until combined. Do not overmix.

- Drop by rounded tablespoons onto ungreased cookie sheets, 1½ inches apart. Bake for 18 to 22 minutes or until the bottoms of cookies begin to brown. Transfer the cookies with a spatula to a cool, flat surface.

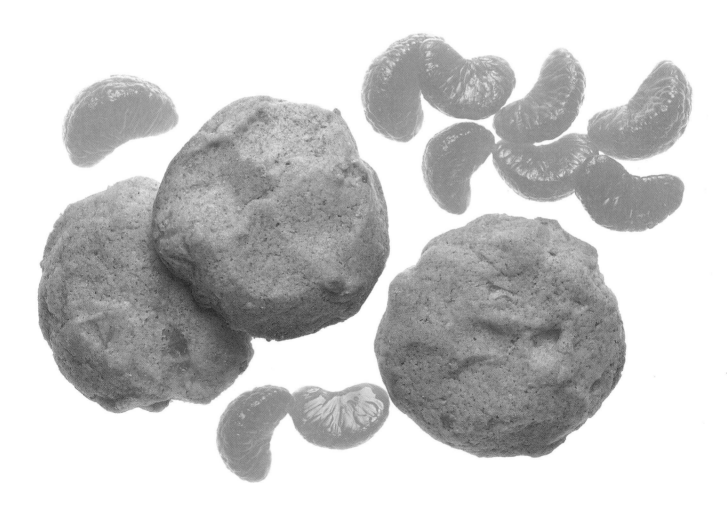

Best White Chocolate Butterscotch Cookies

2½ cups all-purpose flour
1 teaspoon baking soda
¼ teaspoon salt
2 sticks (1 cup) unsalted butter, softened
1½ cups (packed) dark brown sugar
2 large eggs
1 tablespoon light molasses

2 teaspoons vanilla extract
1 teaspoon Scotch whisky
1 cup chopped pecans, toasted
¾ cup butterscotch chips
¾ cup white chocolate chips

Yield: About 3 dozen

- Preheat the oven to 300°F.

- In a medium bowl, combine the flour, baking soda, and salt.

- In a large bowl with an electric mixer, cream the butter and sugar. Add the eggs, molasses, vanilla, and whisky, then blend well. Add the flour mixture and mix to blend. Stir in the pecans, butterscotch chips, and white chocolate chips. Do not overmix.

- Drop the cookie dough by rounded tablespoons 2 inches apart onto an ungreased cookie sheet. Bake for 18 to 20 minutes, or until set. Transfer to wire racks to cool.

Monster Chunk Cookies

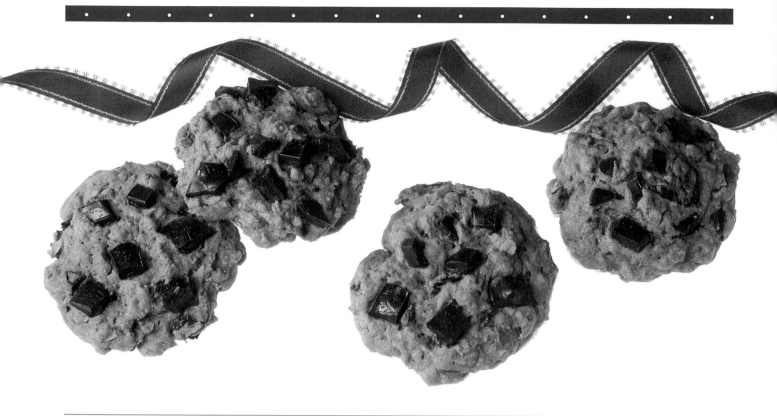

2 cups all-purpose flour
1 cup old-fashioned rolled oats
½ teaspoon baking soda
¼ teaspoon salt
2 sticks (1 cup) unsalted butter, softened
1⅓ cups (packed) dark brown sugar

2 large eggs
2 teaspoons vanilla extract
12 ounces semisweet chocolate, cut into
   large chunks

Yield: 15 large cookies

- Preheat the oven to 300°F. In a medium bowl, combine the flour, oats, baking soda, and salt.

- In a large bowl with an electric mixer, cream the butter. Beat in the sugar and continue to beat until well combined. Beat in the eggs, one at a time, then add the vanilla. On low speed, blend in the flour mixture, stirring in the last bit with a wooden spoon. Stir in the chocolate chunks.

- Divide the dough into 15 equal portions. Place the portions of dough 3 inches apart on an ungreased cookie sheet and pat into disks ½ inch thick.

- Bake for 20 to 22 minutes, or until lightly browned on the underside. Cool on the cookie sheet for 1 minute, then carefully transfer to a wire rack to cool completely.

Before baking, press each mound of cookie dough to a ½-inch thickness.

38

Apricot Nectar Cookies

2¾ cups all-purpose flour
1 teaspoon baking soda
¾ cup granulated sugar
¼ cup (packed) dark brown sugar
2 sticks (1 cup) salted butter, softened
1 large egg

¼ cup apricot nectar
½ cup apricot preserves
¾ cup dried apricots, chopped

Yield: About 2 dozen

- Preheat oven to 300°F.

- In a medium bowl, combine flour and baking soda. Mix well with a wire whisk and set aside.

- In a large bowl, blend sugars with an electric mixer at medium speed. Add butter and mix to form a grainy paste. Scrape down sides of bowl. Then add egg, apricot nectar, and apricot preserves; beat at medium speed until smooth.

- Add the flour mixture and apricots, and blend on low just until combined. Do not overmix.

- Drop by rounded tablespoons onto ungreased cookie sheets, 1½ inches apart. Bake for 19 to 22 minutes or until the cookies just begin to brown at the bottom edges.

- Remove from oven and let cookies cool on cookie sheets 5 minutes before transferring to a cool, flat surface with a spatula.

Cholesterol-Free Chocolate Chip Cookies

2½ cups all-purpose flour
½ teaspoon baking soda
¼ teaspoon salt
¾ cup (packed) dark brown sugar
½ cup granulated sugar
½ cup margarine
3 large egg whites

2 tablespoons honey
2 teaspoons vanilla extract
12 ounces semisweet chocolate chips
  (about 2 cups)

Yield: About 3½ dozen

- Preheat oven to 300°F.

- In medium bowl, combine flour, soda, and salt. Mix well with a wire whisk and set aside.

- In a large bowl, blend sugars with an electric mixer. Add margarine and mix to form a grainy paste.

- In small bowl, beat egg whites until fluffy. Add egg whites, honey, and vanilla to sugar mixture, and beat until smooth. Scrape down the sides of the bowl.

- Add the flour mixture and chocolate chips, and blend on low speed just until combined. Do not overmix.

- Drop by rounded tablespoons onto ungreased cookie sheets, 1½ inches apart. Bake for 15 to 18 minutes until lightly browned. Immediately transfer cookies with a spatula to a cool, flat surface.

Lacy Oatmeal Cookies

1 cup quick oats (not instant)
¼ cup all-purpose flour
½ teaspoon salt
1½ teaspoons baking powder
1 cup granulated sugar

1 stick (½ cup) salted butter, softened
1 large egg
1 teaspoon vanilla extract

Yield: About 8 dozen

- Preheat oven to 325°F. Cover cookie sheets with foil, then coat with nonstick vegetable spray.

- In a medium bowl, combine oats, flour, salt, and baking powder. Mix well with a wire whisk and set aside.

- In a large bowl, combine sugar and butter with an electric mixer at medium speed to form a grainy paste. Add egg and vanilla, and beat until smooth.

Add flour mixture and blend just until combined.

- Drop dough by teaspoons onto cookie sheets, 2½ inches apart. Bake for 9 to 12 minutes or until edges begin to turn golden brown. Let cool, then peel off cookies with your fingers.

- Be sure to respray the cookie sheets between batches.

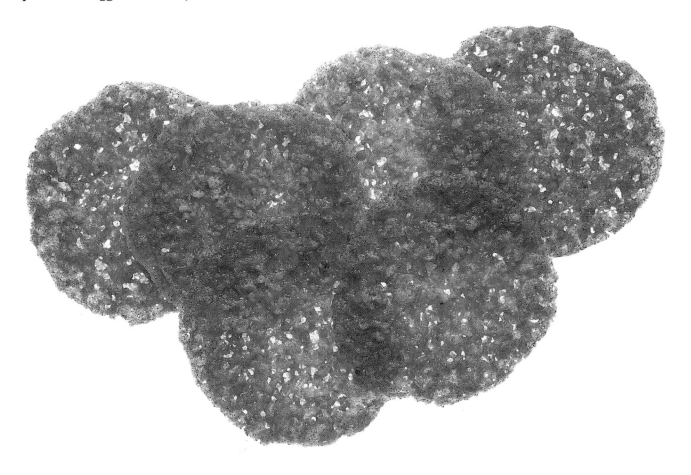

Cocomia Cookies

2 cups all-purpose flour
½ teaspoon baking soda
¼ teaspoon salt
¾ cup (packed) brown sugar
½ cup granulated sugar
1½ sticks (¾ cup) salted butter, softened
2 large eggs

2 teaspoons vanilla extract
6 ounces shredded, unsweetened coconut
 (about 1 cup)
7 ounces whole macadamia nuts
 (about 1½ cups)

Yield: About 3 dozen

- Preheat oven to 300°F.

- In a medium bowl, combine flour, soda, and salt. Mix well with a wire whisk and set aside.

- In a large bowl, blend sugars with an electric mixer at medium speed. Add butter and mix to form a grainy paste. Scrape down sides of bowl, then add eggs and vanilla. Beat at medium speed until light and fluffy.

- Add the flour mixture, the coconut, and macadamia nuts, and blend at low speed just until combined. Do not overmix.

- Drop by rounded tablespoons onto ungreased cookie sheets, 2 inches apart. Bake for 22 to 24 minutes. Immediately transfer cookies with a spatula to a cool, flat surface.

Chippity Chippers

2¾ cups cake flour
1 teaspoon baking soda
½ teaspoon salt
2 sticks (1 cup) unsalted butter, softened
½ cup (packed) light brown sugar
½ cup granulated sugar
1 tablespoon honey
2 large eggs
2 teaspoons vanilla extract
6 ounces semisweet chocolate chips
  (about 1 cup)

6 ounces milk chocolate chips
  (about 1 cup)
6 ounces white chocolate chips
  (about 1 cup)
3 ounces peanut butter chips
  (about ½ cup)

Yield: About 3 dozen

- Preheat the oven to 325°F.

- In a medium bowl, combine the flour, baking soda, and salt.

- In another medium bowl, cream the butter, sugars, and honey. Add the eggs one at a time, beating well after each addition. Beat in the vanilla. Stir in the flour mixture and all of the chips. Stir just until blended; do not overmix.

- Drop the dough by rounded tablespoons 2 inches apart onto an ungreased cookie sheet. Bake for 18 to 20 minutes. Transfer to wire racks to cool.

Chocolate Chip Cookies with Toasted Pecans

2½ cups all-purpose flour
1 teaspoon baking soda
¼ teaspoon salt
2 sticks (1 cup) unsalted butter, softened
1 cup (packed) dark brown sugar
½ cup granulated sugar
2 large eggs

2 teaspoons vanilla extract
1 cup chopped pecans, toasted
12 ounces semisweet chocolate chips
  (about 2 cups)

Yield: About 3 dozen

- Preheat the oven to 300°F.

- In a medium bowl, combine the flour, baking soda, and salt.

- In a large bowl with an electric mixer, cream the butter and sugars. Beat in the eggs and vanilla until just combined.

- Add the flour mixture, toasted pecans, and chocolate chips, then beat on low speed until just blended.

- Drop the dough by rounded tablespoons 2 inches apart onto an ungreased cookie sheet. Bake for 15 to 20 minutes, or until golden. Transfer to wire racks to cool.

Applesauce Oaties

1¾ cups quick oats (not instant)
1½ cups all-purpose flour
1 teaspoon baking powder
½ teaspoon baking soda
½ teaspoon salt
1 teaspoon ground cinnamon
½ teaspoon ground nutmeg
1 cup (packed) light brown sugar
½ cup granulated sugar

1 stick (½ cup) salted butter, softened
1 large egg
¾ cup applesauce
6 ounces semisweet chocolate chips
  (about 1 cup)
6 ounces raisins (about 1 cup)
4 ounces chopped walnuts (about 1 cup)

Yield: About 4 dozen

- Preheat oven to 375°F.

- In a medium bowl, combine oats, flour, baking powder, soda, salt, cinnamon, and nutmeg. Mix well with a wire whisk and set aside.

- In a large bowl, combine sugars with an electric mixer at medium speed. Add butter and beat to form a grainy paste. Add egg and applesauce, and blend until smooth.

- Add the flour mixture, chocolate chips, raisins, and walnuts. Blend at low speed just until combined. Do not overmix.

- Drop dough by tablespoons onto lightly greased cookie sheets, 2 inches apart. Bake for 12 to 14 minutes or until cookies are light brown. Immediately transfer them with a spatula to a cool, flat surface.

Creamy Lemon Macadamia Cookies

2 cups all-purpose flour
½ teaspoon baking soda
¼ teaspoon salt
1 cup (packed) light brown sugar
½ cup granulated sugar
1 stick (½ cup) salted butter, softened
4 ounces cream cheese, softened

1 large egg
2 teaspoons lemon extract
7 ounces whole macadamia nuts
  (about 1½ cups)

Yield: About 2½ dozen

● Preheat oven to 300°F.

● In a medium bowl, combine flour, soda, and salt. Mix well with wire whisk. Set aside.

● In a large bowl, blend sugars well with an electric mixer set at medium speed. Add the butter and cream cheese, and mix to form a smooth paste. Add the egg and lemon extract, and beat at medium speed until fully combined. Scrape down sides of bowl occasionally.

● Add the flour mixture and macadamia nuts. Blend at low speed just until combined. Do not overmix.

● Drop by rounded tablespoons onto ungreased cookie sheets, 2 inches apart. Bake for 18 to 20 minutes. Immediately transfer cookies with a spatula to a cool, flat surface.

Chocolate Crispy Cookies

2 cups all-purpose flour
¼ teaspoon salt
½ teaspoon baking soda
½ cup (packed) dark brown sugar
½ cup granulated sugar
1½ sticks (¾ cup) salted butter, softened
1 large egg

2 teaspoons vanilla extract
1 cup crispy rice cereal
8 ounces crispy rice chocolate bar, coarsely
  chopped (about 1½ cups)

Yield: About 3 dozen

- Preheat oven to 300°F.

- In a medium bowl, combine flour, salt, and soda. Mix well with a wire whisk and set aside.

- In a large bowl, blend sugars with an electric mixer at medium speed. Add butter and mix to form a grainy paste. Scrape down sides of bowl, then add egg and vanilla. Beat at medium speed until light and fluffy.

- Add flour mixture, rice cereal, and chocolate chunks. Blend at low speed just until combined. Do not overmix.

- Drop by rounded tablespoons onto ungreased cookie sheets, 2 inches apart. Bake for 18 to 20 minutes. Immediately transfer cookies with a spatula to a cool, flat surface.

Fudge Cookies with White Chocolate

12 ounces semisweet chocolate, finely chopped
2 cups all-purpose flour
¾ cup unsweetened cocoa powder
1 teaspoon baking soda
¼ teaspoon salt
2 sticks (1 cup) unsalted butter, softened
1½ cups (packed) dark brown sugar

3 large eggs, at room temperature
2 teaspoons vanilla extract
4 ounces white chocolate, coarsely chopped
1 teaspoon vegetable oil

Yield: About 3 dozen

- Preheat the oven to 300°F.

- In a double boiler, melt the semisweet chocolate over hot, not simmering, water. Set aside to cool slightly.

- In a medium bowl, combine the flour, cocoa, baking soda, and salt.

- In a large bowl with an electric mixer, cream the butter and sugar. Beat in the eggs and vanilla until just combined. Blend in the cooled semisweet chocolate. Blend in the flour mixture until just combined.

- Drop the dough by rounded tablespoons 2 inches apart onto an ungreased cookie sheet. Bake for 18 to 22 minutes, or until set. Cool on the cookie sheet for 1 minute, then transfer to wire racks to cool completely.

- In a double boiler, melt the white chocolate with the oil over hot, not simmering, water. Set aside to cool slightly.

- Dip a fork into the melted white chocolate and drizzle over the cookies.

Nutty White Chunk Cookies

2¼ cups all-purpose flour
½ teaspoon baking soda
¼ teaspoon salt
1 cup (packed) light brown sugar
½ cup granulated sugar
1½ sticks (¾ cup) salted butter, softened
2 large eggs

2 teaspoons vanilla extract
4 ounces pecans, chopped (about 1 cup)
8 ounces white chocolate bar,
 coarsely chopped (about 1½ cups)

Yield: About 3 dozen

- Preheat oven to 300°F.

- In medium bowl, combine flour, soda, and salt. Mix well with a wire whisk. Set aside.

- In large bowl with an electric mixer blend sugars at medium speed. Add butter and mix to form a grainy paste, scraping down the sides of the bowl. Add eggs and vanilla, and beat at medium speed until light and fluffy.

- Add the flour mixture, pecans, and white chocolate, and blend at low speed until just combined. Do not overmix.

- Drop by rounded tablespoons onto ungreased cookie sheets, 2 inches apart. Bake for 20 to 22 minutes or until edges just begin to turn golden brown. Use a spatula to transfer cookies immediately to a cool, flat surface.

Pineapple Paradise Cookies

3 cups all-purpose flour
½ teaspoon baking soda
¾ cup (packed) dark brown sugar
¾ cup granulated sugar
2 sticks (1 cup) salted butter, softened
1 large egg
2 teaspoons vanilla extract

One 8-ounce can crushed pineapple or
  1 cup fresh finely chopped pineapple,
  well drained
1 tablespoon pineapple juice
¼ cup sweetened shredded coconut

Yield: About 3 dozen

- Preheat oven to 300°F.

- In medium bowl, combine flour and baking soda. Mix well with a wire whisk. Set aside.

- In large bowl with an electric mixer blend sugars. Add butter and mix to form a grainy paste, scraping down the sides of the bowl. Add egg, vanilla, crushed pineapple, and pineapple juice and beat on medium speed until smooth.

- Add the flour mixture and blend at low speed until just combined. Do not overmix.

- Drop by rounded tablespoons onto ungreased cookie sheets, 2 inches apart. Sprinkle lightly with shredded coconut.

- Bake for 22 to 24 minutes or until cookies begin to turn lightly brown at edges. Transfer immediately to a cool, flat surface with a spatula.

Butterscotch Pecan Cookies

COOKIES
2½ cups all-purpose flour
½ teaspoon baking soda
¼ teaspoon salt
1½ cups (packed) dark brown sugar
2 sticks (1 cup) salted butter, softened
2 large eggs
2 teaspoons vanilla extract*
4 ounces chopped pecans (about 1 cup)
3 ounces whole pecans (about 1 cup)

CARAMEL GLAZE
8 ounces caramels
¼ cup heavy cream

Yield: About 2½ dozen

*For an authentic butterscotch flavor, an
 equal quantity of Scotch whisky may be
 substituted for the vanilla.

- Preheat oven to 300°F.

- In medium bowl, combine flour, soda, and salt. Mix well with a wire whisk. Set aside.

- In large bowl with electric mixer beat sugar and butter. Mix to form a grainy paste, scraping down the sides of the bowl. Add eggs and vanilla, and beat at medium speed until soft and lumpy. Add the flour mixture and chopped pecans, and mix at low speed until just combined. Do not overmix.

- Drop dough by rounded tablespoons 2 inches apart onto ungreased cookie sheets. Place one whole pecan in center of each cookie. Bake for 23 to 25 minutes or until cookie edges begin to brown lightly. Transfer immediately to cool, flat surface with a spatula.

- Prepare the caramel glaze: Melt the caramels with the cream in a small saucepan over low heat. Stir with a wooden spoon until smooth. Remove from heat.

- Drizzle cooled cookies with caramel glaze into desired pattern using a spoon or fork.

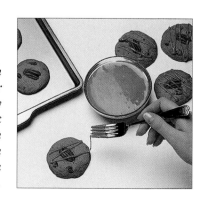

Drizzle cookies with the caramel glaze for an extra touch of creamy flavor. Make sure that the glaze flows from the fork in a thin stream in order to achieve a decorative effect.

Lemon Poppy Seed Cookies

2 cups all-purpose flour
½ teaspoon baking soda
1½ teaspoons freshly grated lemon zest
1 teaspoon ground coriander
2 tablespoons poppy seeds
1½ sticks (¾ cup) salted butter, softened

1 cup granulated sugar
2 large egg yolks
1 large whole egg
1½ teaspoons lemon extract

Yield: About 2 dozen

- Preheat oven 300°F.

- In a medium bowl, combine flour, baking soda, lemon zest, coriander, and poppy seeds. Mix well with a wire whisk and set aside.

- In a large bowl, cream butter and sugar with electric mixer at medium speed until mixture forms a grainy paste. Scrape down sides of bowl, then add yolks, egg, and lemon extract. Beat at medium speed until light and fluffy.

- Add the flour mixture and mix at low speed just until combined. Do not overmix.

- Drop by rounded tablespoons onto ungreased cookie sheets, 2 inches apart. Bake for 21 to 23 minutes until cookies are slightly brown along edges. Immediately transfer cookies with a spatula to a cool, flat surface.

Chocolate Coconut Crunch Cookies

2 cups all-purpose flour
1 teaspoon baking soda
¼ teaspoon salt
2 sticks (1 cup) unsalted butter, softened
¾ cup (packed) light brown sugar
¾ cup granulated sugar
2 large eggs, lightly beaten
2 teaspoons vanilla extract

1 teaspoon almond extract
2 cups shredded coconut
12 ounces semisweet chocolate chips
 (about 2 cups)
1½ cups lightly salted, dry-roasted almonds,
 finely chopped

Yield: About 4 dozen

- Preheat the oven to 300°F.

- In a small bowl, combine the flour, baking soda, and salt.

- In a medium bowl with an electric mixer, cream the butter and sugars. Beat in the eggs, vanilla, and almond extract. Mix on low speed until blended. Add the flour mixture and mix just until blended;

do not overmix. Add the coconut, chocolate chips, and almonds and stir until just incorporated.

- Drop the dough by rounded tablespoons 2 inches apart onto an ungreased cookie sheet. Bake for 18 to 20 minutes, or until set. Transfer to wire racks to cool.

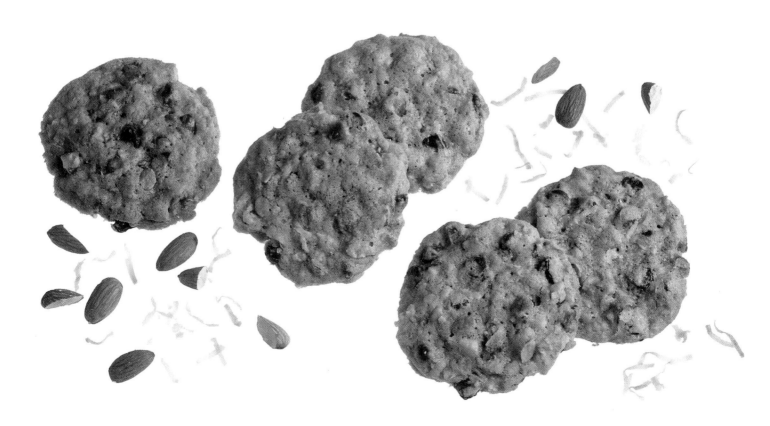

53

Chocolate Peanut Florentines

4 tablespoons (¼ cup) unsalted butter
¼ cup (packed) light brown sugar
¼ cup light corn syrup
⅓ cup all-purpose flour
½ cup finely chopped unsalted peanuts

1 teaspoon vanilla extract
4 ounces semisweet chocolate, finely chopped

Yield: About 16 sandwich cookies

- Preheat the oven to 350°F. Butter and flour a cookie sheet.

- In a small saucepan, melt the butter over medium heat. Add the brown sugar and corn syrup and bring to a boil over medium heat, stirring constantly until the sugar dissolves, 3 to 5 minutes. Remove the pan from the heat and stir in the flour, peanuts, and vanilla.

- Quickly drop the batter in ½-teaspoon mounds 2 inches apart onto the prepared cookie sheet. Using a small spatula, spread each mound into an even circle.

- Bake for 9 to 10 minutes, or until browned; rotate the pan back to front halfway through the baking time. Cool on the cookie sheet for 1 to 2 minutes, then transfer to wire racks to cool completely.

- In a double boiler, melt the chocolate over hot, not simmering, water. Spread a thin layer of chocolate over the bottom (flat side) of one cookie. Cover with another cookie and gently press together. Repeat with the remaining cookies. Refrigerate the cookies to set the chocolate.

Soft and Chewy Peanut Butter Cookies

2 cups all-purpose flour
½ teaspoon baking soda
¼ teaspoon salt
1¼ cups (packed) dark brown sugar
1¼ cups granulated sugar
2 sticks (1 cup) salted butter, softened

3 large eggs
1 cup creamy peanut butter
2 teaspoons vanilla extract

Yield: About 3½ dozen

- Preheat oven to 300°F.

- In a medium bowl, combine flour, soda, and salt. Mix well with a wire whisk. Set aside.

- In a large bowl, blend sugars using an electric mixer set at medium speed. Add butter and mix to form a grainy paste, scraping the sides of the bowl. Add eggs, peanut butter, and vanilla, and mix at medium speed until light and fluffy.

- Add the flour mixture and mix at low speed until just mixed. Do not overmix.

- Drop by rounded tablespoons onto an ungreased cookie sheet, 1½ inches apart. With a wet fork, gently press a crisscross pattern on top of cookies. Bake for 18 to 22 minutes until cookies are slightly brown along edges. Transfer cookies immediately to a cool, flat surface with a spatula.

- As a variation, add 2 cups coarsely chopped semisweet chocolate bar or 2 cups semisweet chocolate chips to the flour mixture, then bake as directed.

After the dough is dropped onto the cookie sheet, use a fork to press a crisscross pattern in each cookie. In order to keep dough from sticking to the fork as you proceed, dip the fork in water after each cookie is flattened.

55

Oatmeal Raisin Chews

2¼ cups all-purpose flour
½ teaspoon baking soda
¼ teaspoon salt
1 cup quick oats (not instant)
1 cup (packed) dark brown sugar
½ cup granulated sugar
2 sticks (1 cup) salted butter, softened
2 tablespoons honey

2 teaspoons vanilla extract
2 large eggs
8 ounces raisins (about 1½ cups)
3 ounces walnuts, chopped (about ½ cup)
  (optional)

Yield: About 2½ dozen without walnuts
  About 3 dozen with walnuts

- Preheat oven to 300°F.

- In a medium bowl, combine flour, soda, salt, and oats. Mix well with wire whisk and set aside.

- In a large bowl, blend sugars with an electric mixer set at medium speed. Add butter and mix to form a grainy paste. Scrape down sides of bowl, then add honey, vanilla, and eggs. Mix at medium speed until light and fluffy.

- Add the flour mixture, raisins, and walnuts, if desired, and blend at low speed just until combined. Do not overmix.

- Drop by rounded tablespoons onto ungreased cookie sheets, 1½ inches apart. Bake for 18 to 22 minutes or until cookies are light golden brown. Immediately transfer cookies with a spatula to a cool, flat surface.

Pumpkin Spice Cookies

2½ cups all-purpose flour
½ teaspoon baking soda
¼ teaspoon salt
2 teaspoons pumpkin pie spice
1 cup (packed) dark brown sugar
½ cup granulated sugar
1½ sticks (¾ cup) salted butter, softened

1 large egg
1 cup pumpkin (canned or freshly cooked)
1 teaspoon vanilla extract
6 ounces raisins (about 1 cup)
2 ounces walnuts, chopped (about ½ cup)

Yield: About 3 dozen

- Preheat oven to 300°F.

- In a medium bowl, combine flour, soda, salt, and pumpkin pie spice. Mix well with a wire whisk and set aside.

- In a large bowl, blend sugars with an electric mixer set at medium speed. Add the butter and beat to form a grainy paste. Scrape sides of bowl, then add egg, pumpkin, and vanilla. Beat at medium speed until light and fluffy.

- Add the flour mixture, raisins, and walnuts. Blend at low speed just until combined. Do not overmix.

- Drop by rounded tablespoons onto ungreased cookie sheets, 1½ inches apart. Bake for 22 to 24 minutes until cookies are slightly brown along edges. Immediately transfer cookies with a spatula to a cool, flat surface.

Chocolate Raisin Cookies

2 sticks (1 cup) salted butter, divided
2 ounces unsweetened baking chocolate
2¼ cups all-purpose flour
½ teaspoon baking soda
¼ teaspoon salt
1 cup (packed) dark brown sugar
½ cup granulated sugar

2 large eggs
2 teaspoons vanilla extract
9 ounces raisins (about 1½ cups)
6 ounces semisweet chocolate chips
  (about 1 cup)

Yield: About 4 dozen

- Preheat oven to 300°F.

- In a double boiler over hot, not boiling, water, melt ½ cup butter and the unsweetened chocolate. Remove from heat. Set aside.

- In a medium bowl, combine flour, soda, and salt. Mix well with a wire whisk. Set aside.

- In a large bowl with an electric mixer blend sugars at medium speed until fluffy. Add the remaining ½ cup butter and mix to form a grainy paste, scraping down the sides of the bowl. Add eggs and vanilla, and beat at medium speed until light and fluffy. Add melted chocolate and blend until the mixture is thoroughly combined.

- Add the flour mixture, raisins, and chocolate chips. Blend at low speed until just combined. Do not overmix.

- Drop by rounded tablespoons onto ungreased cookie sheets, 2 inches apart. Bake for 20 to 22 minutes or until set. Transfer to a cool, flat surface immediately with a spatula.

58

Filled Cookies

Glazed Honey-Nut Rolls

FILLING AND HONEY GLAZE
¾ cup clover honey
⅓ cup water
1 teaspoon fresh lemon juice
1 cinnamon stick
8 ounces walnuts, coarsely chopped
4 ounces raisins (about ¾ cup)
1 teaspoon vanilla extract
¼ teaspoon almond extract
6 ounces semisweet chocolate chips
　(about 1 cup)

ASSEMBLY
10 sheets (13 by 22 inches) frozen phyllo
　dough (about ¼ pound), thawed
1 stick (½ cup) unsalted butter, melted

CHOCOLATE GLAZE
⅓ cup heavy cream
4 ounces semisweet chocolate chips

Powdered sugar, for dusting

Yield: About 20 nut rolls

● Prepare the filling: In a small saucepan, combine the honey, water, lemon juice, and cinnamon. Simmer for 10 minutes. Keep warm.

● In a medium bowl, combine the walnuts, raisins, vanilla, almond extract, and ½ cup of the honey mixture. Stir in the chocolate chips and set aside.

● Assemble and bake: Preheat the oven to 375°F. Keeping the rest of the phyllo covered with plastic wrap and a damp towel, lay a sheet of dough on a work surface. Cut in half crosswise. Brush each half with melted butter. With a short end facing you, spoon about 1½ tablespoons of filling onto the phyllo. Fold in the sides and roll up the dough. Brush the rolls with more butter and place on a cookie sheet. Repeat with the remaining dough, filling, and butter. Bake for 20 minutes, or until golden. Transfer to wire racks to cool, but immediately brush the rolls with the remaining honey glaze.

● Make the chocolate glaze: In a small saucepan, bring the cream to a simmer. Remove from the heat, add the chips, and let stand for 5 minutes; stir until smooth. Let cool, then drizzle over the nut rolls. Dust the rolls with powdered sugar.

With a short end of the phyllo facing you, place about 1½ tablespoons of the filling about 1 inch in from the end. Fold in the sides of the dough and roll up.

Apple Cream Pennies

COOKIES
2½ cups all-purpose flour
½ teaspoon baking soda
¼ teaspoon salt
1 cup (packed) dark brown sugar
½ cup granulated sugar
2 sticks (1 cup) salted butter, softened
2 large eggs

2 teaspoons vanilla extract

FILLING
8 ounces cream cheese, softened
¼ cup granulated sugar
¼ cup apple butter

Yield: About 6 dozen

- Preheat oven to 300°F.

- In a medium bowl, combine flour, soda, and salt. Mix well with a wire whisk. Set aside.

- Blend sugars in a large bowl using an electric mixer set at medium speed. Add butter and mix to form a grainy paste, scraping down the sides of the bowl. Add eggs and vanilla, and beat at medium speed until light and fluffy.

- Add the flour mixture and blend at low speed until just combined. Do not overmix.

- Shape dough into marble-size balls. Place balls on ungreased cookie sheets, 1 inch apart. Bake for 10 to 11 minutes. Do not brown. Transfer cookies to a cool, flat surface with a spatula.

- Prepare the filling: Blend cream cheese and sugar in a medium bowl with an electric mixer on medium until fluffy. Add apple butter and beat until filling is smooth and thoroughly combined.

- With a small knife spread 1 teaspoon of apple cream on the bottom half of each cooled cookie. Top with another cookie to create a sandwich. Repeat with remaining cookies and filling.

Jessica's Marshmallow Clouds

3 cups all-purpose flour
⅔ cup unsweetened cocoa powder
½ teaspoon baking soda
1 cup granulated sugar
1 cup (packed) light brown sugar
2 sticks (1 cup) salted butter, softened
2 large eggs

2 teaspoons vanilla extract
12 ounces mini semisweet chocolate chips
  (about 2 cups)
8 ounces mini marshmallows, frozen

Yield: About 3½ dozen

- Preheat oven to 350°F. Until you are ready to assemble the cookies just prior to baking, keep the marshmallows in the freezer—otherwise they will thaw too rapidly.

- In a medium bowl, combine flour, cocoa, and baking soda. Set aside.

- Combine sugars in a large bowl. Using an electric mixer, blend in butter, scraping down the sides of the bowl. Add eggs and vanilla, and beat at medium speed until light and fluffy.

- Add the flour mixture and chocolate chips, and blend at low speed until combined. Batter will be very stiff.

- Gather 4 or 5 frozen marshmallows in the palm of your hand and cover them with a heaping tablespoon of dough. Wrap the dough around the marshmallows, completely encasing them and forming a 2-inch-diameter dough ball.

- Place balls on ungreased cookie sheets, 2 inches apart. Bake for 10 to 12 minutes. Cool on sheet 2 minutes, then transfer to a cool, flat surface.

Take 4 or 5 frozen mini marshmallows in the palm of your hand (far left). Spoon a heaping tablespoon of dough over the marshmallows and wrap them inside (left). Form a 2-inch ball, then place it on an ungreased cookie sheet.

Lemon Cream-Filled Cookies

COOKIES
1½ sticks (¾ cup) salted butter, softened
½ cup powdered sugar
2 teaspoons lemon extract
1½ cups all-purpose flour
¼ cup cornstarch

FILLING
½ stick (¼ cup) salted butter, softened
1 cup powdered sugar
1 tablespoon heavy cream
Juice of 1 freshly squeezed lemon
  (about 2 tablespoons)
Grated zest of 1 lemon (2 to 3 teaspoons)

Yield: About 2 dozen

- Make the cookie dough: In a medium bowl, cream butter with an electric mixer set at medium speed. Add sugar and beat until smooth, scraping down sides of bowl as needed.

- Add lemon extract and beat until light and fluffy. Then add flour and cornstarch; blend at low speed until thoroughly combined.

- Gather dough into 2 balls of equal size and flatten into disks. Wrap the disks tightly in plastic wrap or a plastic bag. Refrigerate for 1 hour.

- Make the filling: In a small bowl, beat butter with mixer until fluffy. Gradually add sugar while continuing to beat. Add cream, lemon juice, and lemon zest. Mix until thoroughly blended and set aside. To harden filling quickly, refrigerate for 15 to 20 minutes.

- At this point, preheat the oven to 325°F.

- Using a floured rolling pin, roll the chilled cookie dough on a floured board to a ¼-inch thickness. Cut circles with a 2-inch-diameter cookie cutter or drinking glass. Place circles of dough on ungreased cookie sheets, ½ inch apart. Continue rolling out and cutting dough scraps until all dough is used.

- Bake for 15 to 17 minutes, or until edges begin to brown. Immediately transfer cookies with a spatula to a cool, flat surface.

- When cookies are completely cool, spread a cookie with 1 teaspoon of the lemon cream. Place another cookie on top of the filling to make a sandwich. Complete entire batch.

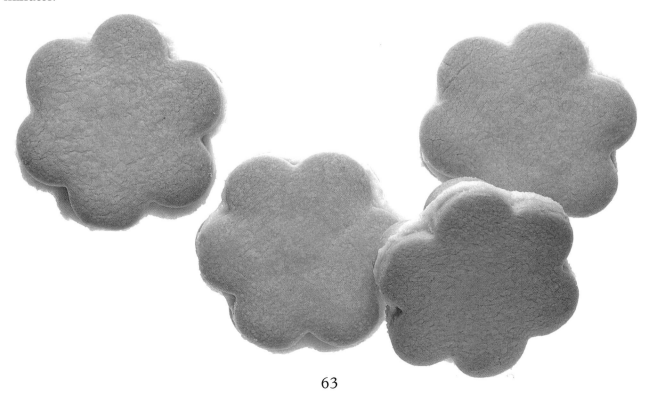

Chocolate Glazed Creamy Lemon Turnovers

PASTRY
2 cups all-purpose flour
2 tablespoons granulated sugar
½ teaspoon salt
1½ sticks (¾ cup) cold unsalted butter, cut
  into pieces
2 ounces cold cream cheese, cut into pieces
3 tablespoons ice water

LEMON FILLING
6 tablespoons unsalted butter
4 large egg yolks

1 large egg
¾ cup granulated sugar
¼ cup fresh lemon juice
2 teaspoons grated lemon peel

TOPPINGS
1 egg, beaten
Granulated sugar, for sprinkling
5 ounces semisweet chocolate chips
½ cup heavy cream

Yield: 2 dozen turnovers

- Prepare the pastry: In a medium bowl, combine the flour, sugar, and salt. With a pastry blender, incorporate the butter and cream cheese until the mixture is the size of small peas. With a fork, stir in the ice water. Gather the dough into a ball, flatten into a disk, wrap in plastic, and chill in the refrigerator for about 30 minutes.

- Make the lemon filling: In a double boiler, melt the butter. In a medium bowl, whisk together the egg yolks, egg, sugar, lemon juice, and lemon peel. Add the egg mixture to the butter and cook, stirring frequently, until the mixture thickens and heavily coats the back of a spoon, about 15 minutes. Transfer the filling to a small bowl and refrigerate until firm, about 2 hours.

- Bake: Preheat the oven to 400°F. Cut the chilled dough in half and return half to the refrigerator. Roll the remaining half into a 12-by-16-inch rectangle. Cut into twelve 4-inch squares. Spoon about 1 tablespoon of filling into the center of each square. Moisten two adjacent sides of a pastry square with water, then fold the pastry over to form a triangle. Crimp the edges to seal. Brush each turnover with some of the beaten egg and cut three slits as steam vents. Sprinkle the tops with granulated sugar and place on an ungreased cookie sheet. Bake for 20 minutes, or until golden. Place on racks to cool to room temperature. Repeat with the remaining dough and filling.

- Meanwhile, make the chocolate glaze: Place the chocolate chips in a small bowl. In a small saucepan, bring the cream to a simmer. Pour the hot cream over the chocolate. Let stand, covered, for 5 minutes, then stir until smooth.

- Drizzle the turnovers with the chocolate glaze.

Pineapple Pocket Pies

COOKIES

1 cup all-purpose flour
½ cup whole-wheat flour
½ teaspoon baking soda
½ stick (¼ cup) salted butter, softened
¼ cup (packed) light brown sugar
¼ cup honey
1 large egg
1 teaspoon vanilla extract

FILLING

½ cup dried apricots
½ cup fresh or canned unsweetened pineapple,
  in chunks
¼ cup (packed) dark brown sugar
1½ cups water

Yield: 32 pockets

- In a medium bowl, combine flours and soda. Mix well with a wire whisk. Set aside.

- In a large bowl with an electric mixer combine butter and sugar at medium speed. Add honey, egg, and vanilla and beat at medium speed until smooth. Scrape down the sides of the bowl, then add the flour mixture. Blend at low speed until just combined; do not overmix.

- Gather dough into a ball. Divide in half and roll into two 6-inch cylinders. Wrap each cylinder tightly in plastic wrap or in a plastic bag. Chill 1 hour.

- Prepare the filling: Combine all the filling ingredients in a medium saucepan over medium-low heat and stir until sugar dissolves. Turn heat up to medium and simmer—stirring occasionally—until mixture thickens and most of the liquid evaporates. Remove from heat and allow mixture to cool to room temperature. Purée filling in food processor or blender.

- Preheat oven to 325°F. Using your hands, roll each cylinder out to about 12 inches in length. Then place 1 cylinder on a floured board and using a floured rolling pin, roll into a rectangle roughly 5 inches wide, 18 inches long, and ⅛ inch thick.

- Spread half of the filling mixture down the center of the dough in a ribbon about 2 inches wide. With a metal spatula, loosen the dough, and fold each side lengthwise over the filling, one side overlapping the other by ½ inch.

- Cut strip in half widthwise. Use spatula to transfer each 9-inch strip onto an ungreased cookie sheet, turning the strips over so the seams are on the bottom. Repeat with remaining dough and filling.

- Bake for 20 to 22 minutes or until dough begins to turn a light gold. Do not brown. Cool strips on sheet for 1 minute, then transfer to a cool surface. When strips reach room temperature, cut each into 8 pieces with a thin, sharp knife.

Refrigerator Thumbprint Fudgy Cookies

½ stick (¼ cup) salted butter, softened
½ cup heavy cream
1 cup granulated sugar
1 teaspoon vanilla extract
12 ounces semisweet chocolate chips
    (about 2 cups)

2½ cups quick oats (not instant)
1 cup raspberry preserves
¼ cup powdered sugar

Yield: About 2½ dozen

- In a 2-quart saucepan, combine butter, cream, and sugar. Warm over medium heat, stirring constantly, until sugar dissolves. Remove from heat, add vanilla and chocolate chips, 1 cup at a time, stirring until chocolate melts. To complete the dough, fold in the oats and stir until all ingredients are thoroughly combined.

- Shape dough into 1-inch balls and place on a cookie sheet lined with wax paper. Using the bottom of a glass, flatten cookies to 2 inches in diameter. Make a depression in center of each cookie with your thumb. Chill cookies in refrigerator 30 minutes or until set. Spoon ½ teaspoon of preserves into center of each cookie. Dust with powdered sugar.

Spoon the chocolate chips into the liquid ingredients 1 cup at a time (far left). Stir after each addition to ensure that the chips have melted. After all the chocolate has been incorporated, add the oats and stir until completely moistened (left).

Surprise-Filled Cookies

2½ *cups all-purpose flour*
½ *teaspoon baking powder*
2 sticks (1 cup) salted butter, softened
1 cup granulated sugar
1 large egg

2 teaspoons vanilla extract
1 cup fruit jam

Yield: About 4 dozen

- Preheat oven to 300°F.

- In a medium bowl, combine flour and baking powder. Mix well with a wire whisk. Set aside.

- In another medium bowl with an electric mixer, cream butter and sugar. Add egg and vanilla, and beat on medium until smooth. Add the flour mixture and blend at low speed until thoroughly combined. Dough will be firm.

- Scoop tablespoonfuls of dough, roll into 1-inch-diameter balls, and place on ungreased cookie sheets, 1 inch apart. With the small end of a melon baller, scoop out the center of the dough balls. Do not scoop all the way through the cookie. Place ½ teaspoon of jam in the center of each dough ball. Place scooped-out dough back into mixing bowl to use to form more cookies.

- Bake for 22 to 24 minutes or until golden brown. Transfer to a cool, flat surface.

Use the smaller scoop of a melon baller to remove a small amount of dough from each ball. Spoon your favorite jams into the depression, then bake as directed.

Peanut Butter Cream-Filled Cookies

COOKIES

1½ cups all-purpose flour
½ teaspoon baking soda
½ teaspoon ground cinnamon
1 cup quick oats (not instant)
1 cup (packed) light brown sugar
1 stick (½ cup) salted butter, softened
1 large egg
1 teaspoon vanilla extract

FILLING

¾ cup creamy peanut butter
½ stick (¼ cup) salted butter, softened
2 tablespoons half-and-half
1 teaspoon vanilla extract
1½ cups powdered sugar

Yield: About 3½ dozen

- Preheat oven to 325°F.

- In a medium bowl, combine flour, soda, cinnamon, and oats. Mix well with a wire whisk. Set aside.

- Cream sugar and butter in a large bowl using an electric mixer set at medium speed. Add egg and vanilla, and beat at medium speed until light and creamy. Add the flour-oat mixture, and blend at low speed until just combined. Do not overmix.

- Separate dough into 2 balls, flatten them into disks, and wrap each tightly in plastic wrap or a plastic bag. Chill for 1 hour.

- On floured board using a floured rolling pin, roll out 1 disk to ¼-inch thickness. Cut cookies with a 2-inch round fluted cookie cutter dipped in flour. Repeat procedure with the second disk, reworking scraps until all the dough is used. Bake cookies on ungreased cookie sheets ½ inch apart for 13 to 15 minutes or until bottoms turn light brown. Transfer immediately to a cool, flat surface with a spatula.

- When cookies are cool, mix filling ingredients and spread 1 tablespoon of peanut butter filling on the bottom side of a cookie. Top with another cookie—bottom side toward the filling—to make a sandwich. Repeat with the remaining cookies and filling.

Use a cookie cutter dipped in flour to cut the cookies from the dough. This cookie cutter has a fluted edge—it makes a particularly attractive cookie.

Chocolate Cream-Filled Hearts

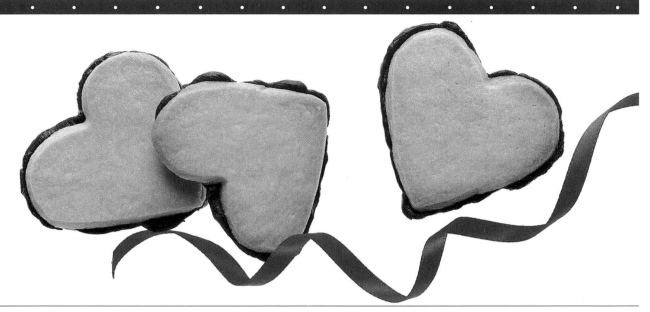

COOKIES
3 sticks (1½ cups) salted butter, softened
1½ cups powdered sugar
4 teaspoons vanilla extract
3 cups all-purpose flour

CHOCOLATE CREAM FILLING
½ cup heavy cream
6 ounces semisweet chocolate chips
  (about 1 cup)

TOPPING
¼ cup powdered sugar (optional)

Yield: About 2½ dozen

- Cream butter in a medium bowl with electric mixer set at medium speed. Add 1½ cups powdered sugar and beat until smooth. Add vanilla and mix until creamy. Scrape bowl. Add flour and mix at low speed until thoroughly mixed.

- Gather dough into 2 balls and flatten into disks. Wrap dough tightly in plastic wrap or place in an airtight plastic bag. Refrigerate for 1 hour or until firm.

- Preheat oven to 325°F.

- Using a floured rolling pin, roll dough on floured board to ¼-inch thickness. Cut out 2-inch hearts with cookie cutters. Continue using dough scraps, rerolling and recutting until all dough is used. Be careful not to overwork the dough.

- Place cookies on ungreased cookie sheets, ½ inch apart. Bake for 16 to 18 minutes or until firm. Transfer to cool, flat surface with spatula.

- Prepare the chocolate cream filling: Scald the cream in a small saucepan and remove from heat.

Stir in the chocolate chips and cover for 15 minutes. Stir chocolate cream until smooth, then transfer to a small bowl. Set filling aside and let it cool to room temperature.

- Spread 1 teaspoon of chocolate filling on the bottom side of half of the cookies. Top with bottom side of another cookie, forming a sandwich. Repeat with remaining cookies and cream.

- If you wish, sift powdered sugar over the finished cookies.

Spread the chocolate filling on the bottom side of one cookie heart. Top with another heart, bottom side also touching the chocolate.

Chocolate Sandwich Cookies

COOKIES
1½ sticks (¾ cup) salted butter, softened
¾ cup powdered sugar
2 teaspoons vanilla extract
¼ cup unsweetened cocoa powder
2 tablespoons cornstarch
1 cup all-purpose flour

CREAM FILLING
1 stick (½ cup) salted butter, softened
1 cup powdered sugar
2 teaspoons vanilla extract
1 tablespoon heavy cream

Yield: About 1½ dozen

- In a medium bowl, cream butter with an electric mixer at medium speed. Add sugar and beat until smooth. Add vanilla and beat at medium speed until light and fluffy. In another bowl, combine the cocoa, cornstarch, and flour, and mix well with a wire whisk. Add the cocoa mixture to the wet ingredients and mix at low speed until thoroughly combined.

- Gather dough into a ball and flatten into a disk. Wrap dough tightly in plastic wrap or place in an airtight plastic bag. Refrigerate for 1½ hours or until firm.

- Preheat oven to 325°F.

- Using a floured rolling pin, roll dough on floured board to ¼-inch thickness. Cut shapes with cookie cutters and place on ungreased cookie sheets, 1 inch apart. Continue using dough scraps, rerolling and cutting until all dough is used. Be careful not to overwork the dough. Bake for 16 to 18 minutes or until firm. Transfer cookies to a cool, flat surface with a spatula.

- Prepare the cream filling: Cream butter in a small bowl with an electric mixer set at medium speed. Add sugar, vanilla, and cream, and beat until smooth.

- Spread 1½ teaspoons of cream filling on the bottom sides of half of the cookies. Top with the remaining cookies.

Custard-Filled Cookies

CUSTARD
1 cup sweetened condensed milk
One ½-inch piece vanilla bean, split lengthwise, or 1 teaspoon vanilla extract
2 large egg yolks, at room temperature

COOKIES
1 stick (½ cup) salted butter, softened
½ cup granulated sugar
1 large egg

2 tablespoons heavy cream
1½ cups all-purpose flour

TOPPINGS
1 teaspoon ground cinnamon or
1 teaspoon powdered sugar or
1 teaspoon cocoa powder

Yield: About 1½ dozen

- In a medium saucepan over medium heat, heat condensed milk with vanilla bean or vanilla extract until small bubbles form on surface.

- Whisk egg yolks in a medium bowl. Stirring constantly, slowly add ½ cup of the hot milk to the egg yolks. Add the tempered egg yolks to the milk mixture in the saucepan. Stirring constantly with a metal spoon or whisk, cook for 5 minutes or until custard heavily coats the back of a spoon. Be careful not to let the custard boil.

- Strain custard through a sieve. Refrigerate until thoroughly chilled.

- Preheat oven to 325°F.

- Prepare the cookies: Mix butter and sugar in medium bowl with electric mixer at medium speed. Add egg and cream and mix until thoroughly blended. Scrape sides of bowl. Add the flour and blend on low speed just until combined. Do not overmix.

- Shape dough into 1-inch balls and place on ungreased cookie sheets 1 inch apart. With your thumb or the back of a small spoon, form a small depression in center of each ball.

- Bake for 15 to 17 minutes or until bottoms begin to brown. Transfer cookies to cool, flat surface. When cookies cool to room temperature, spoon or pipe in 1½ teaspoons of chilled thickened custard. Sprinkle with ground cinnamon, powdered sugar, or cocoa, if desired.

Temper the beaten egg yolks by adding about ½ cup of the hot milk to the yolks, briskly whisking as you pour. This will warm the eggs enough so that when you add them to the hot milk, they will not become scrambled eggs.

71

Linzer Cookies

COOKIES
1½ cups all-purpose flour
½ cup ground almonds
½ teaspoon baking powder
¼ teaspoon salt
½ teaspoon ground cinnamon
1½ sticks (¾ cup) salted butter, softened
¾ cup granulated sugar
2 egg yolks
1 teaspoon vanilla extract
1 teaspoon almond extract

FILLING
½ cup raspberry jam
1 teaspoon grated lemon peel
 (½ of 1 medium lemon)

TOPPING
¼ cup powdered sugar
2 ounces sliced almonds (about ½ cup)

Yield: About 2 dozen

- Preheat oven to 300°F.
- Combine flour, almonds, baking powder, salt, and cinnamon with wire whisk.
- In a large bowl with an electric mixer cream butter and sugar. Add egg yolks and the vanilla and almond extracts, and beat at medium speed until light and fluffy. Add the flour mixture and blend at low speed until just combined. Do not overmix.
- Roll dough into 1½-inch balls. Place 2 inches apart on ungreased cookie sheets. With your index finger press an indentation in center of each ball to hold the filling.
- Bake for 22 to 24 minutes or until just golden brown on bottom. Transfer cookies to a cool, flat surface with a spatula.
- In a small bowl, combine jam and grated lemon peel. Sift powdered sugar over cookies. Place ½ teaspoon of filling mixture in center of cooled cookie and place sliced almonds in the jam filling.

Once the cookies are cool, lightly dust them with powdered sugar (far left). Next, spoon the raspberry jam into the depression in each cookie. To finish off, arrange sliced almonds on top of the jam (left).

Fruit-Filled Jewels

1½ sticks (¾ cup) salted butter, softened
½ cup powdered sugar
2 large egg yolks
1 teaspoon vanilla extract

1½ cups all-purpose flour
1 cup any fruit jam

Yield: About 2 dozen

- Preheat oven to 325°F.

- In a medium bowl, cream butter with an electric mixer set at medium speed. Add sugar and beat until smooth. Add egg yolks and vanilla, and beat at medium speed until light and fluffy. Add the flour and blend at low speed until thoroughly combined.

- Gather dough into a ball and flatten into a disk. Wrap dough tightly in plastic wrap or place in plastic bag. Refrigerate for 1 hour.

- Using a floured rolling pin, roll dough on floured board to ¼-inch thickness. Cut circles with a 2-inch-diameter cookie cutter or drinking glass, and place on ungreased cookie sheets, 1 inch apart. Continue using dough scraps, rerolling and cutting until all the dough is used.

- Drop ½ teaspoon of fruit jam in center of each cookie, then top with another cookie. Using the tines of a fork, seal edges of cookies as shown.

- Bake for 15 to 17 minutes or until edges begin to brown.

Chocolate Dreams

COOKIES
1½ sticks (¾ cup) salted butter, softened
½ cup powdered sugar
¼ cup (packed) light brown sugar
2 large egg yolks
1 teaspoon vanilla extract
1½ cups all-purpose flour

CHOCOLATE FILLING
½ cup heavy cream
6 ounces semisweet chocolate chips
  (about 1 cup)

TOPPING
2 tablespoons granulated sugar

Yield: About 2½ dozen

- In a medium bowl, cream butter using an electric mixer set at medium speed. Add powdered and brown sugars and beat until smooth. Add yolks and vanilla, and mix at medium speed until light and fluffy. Scrape bowl. Add the flour and blend at low speed until thoroughly combined.

- Gather dough into a ball and flatten into a disk. Wrap dough tightly in plastic wrap or place in plastic bag. Refrigerate for 1 hour.

- Prepare the filling: Scald the cream in a small saucepan over medium heat. Add the chocolate chips and stir until melted. Remove from the heat.

- Preheat oven to 325°F.

- Using a floured rolling pin, roll dough on floured board to ¼-inch thickness. Cut circles with a 2-inch-diameter cookie cutter and place on ungreased cookie sheets, 1 inch apart. Continue using dough scraps, rerolling and cutting until all dough is used. Drop 1 teaspoon of chocolate filling in center of each circle and top with another circle. Completely seal the edges using the tines of a fork. Bake for 15 to 16 minutes, or until cookies are golden brown. Transfer cookies to a cool, flat surface with a metal spatula. Sprinkle with granulated sugar.

Spoon a heaping teaspoonful of chocolate filling into the center of each circle (far left). Cover each with another circle of dough and completely seal the edges with a fork (left).

Fancy Cookies

Almond Crunch Cookies

1 stick (½ cup) salted butter, softened
¾ cup granulated sugar
1 large egg
½ teaspoon almond extract
1 ounce almonds, ground in blender or food
  processor (about ¼ cup)
4 ounces sliced almonds (about 1 cup)

1 cup all-purpose flour
¼ cup heavy cream
6 ounces semisweet chocolate chips
  (about 1 cup)
2 teaspoons light corn syrup

Yield: About 1½ dozen

- Preheat oven to 350°F.

- In a medium bowl, blend butter and sugar with an electric mixer until mixture forms a grainy paste. Scrape down sides of bowl, then add egg and almond extract. Beat at medium speed until light and fluffy.

- Add the ground almonds and flour, and blend at low speed just until combined. Do not overmix. Form dough into 1½-inch balls and roll in sliced almonds, coating each ball thoroughly.

- Place balls on ungreased cookie sheets, 2 inches apart. Bake for 15 to 18 minutes or until cookies are slightly brown along edges. Immediately trans-fer cookies to a cool surface covered with wax paper.

- Make the chocolate glaze: Scald cream in a small saucepan, then remove from heat. Stir in chocolate chips and corn syrup; cover and let stand for 15 minutes. With small wire whisk or wooden spoon, gently mix glaze until smooth, being careful not to create bubbles in the chocolate.

- When cookies are completely cool, drizzle patterns on them with the warm chocolate glaze, or dip half of each cookie into the glaze. Refrigerate the cookies on the wax paper until the glaze has set—about 10 minutes.

Roll dough lightly between your hands into 1½-inch balls. The less you handle these cookies the lighter they will be.

Then roll each ball in sliced almonds until fully coated.

77

Molasses Raisin Cookies

COOKIES
3¼ cups all-purpose flour
1 teaspoon baking soda
¼ teaspoon salt
2 teaspoons ground cinnamon
1 teaspoon ground ginger
½ teaspoon allspice
1 cup (packed) dark brown sugar
2 sticks (1 cup) salted butter, softened

¾ cup unsulfurized molasses
1 large egg
6 ounces raisins (about 1½ cups)

ICING
1 cup powdered sugar
2 tablespoons milk

Yield: About 4 dozen

- Preheat oven to 300°F.

- In a medium bowl, combine flour, soda, salt, cinnamon, ginger, and allspice. Mix well with a wire whisk and set aside.

- In a large bowl, beat sugar and butter with an electric mixer at medium speed until mixture forms a grainy paste. Scrape sides of bowl, then add molasses and egg. Beat until light and fluffy.

- Add the flour mixture and raisins, and blend at low speed just until combined. Do not overmix.

- Divide dough in half and shape each half into a roll 1½ inches in diameter. Wrap rolls in wax paper and refrigerate until firm, about 2 hours.

- Slice cookies ½ inch thick and place on ungreased cookie sheets, 1½ inches apart. Bake for 25 to 27 minutes until cookies are set.

- Immediately transfer cookies with a spatula to a cool surface.

- Prepare the icing: Blend sugar and milk in a small bowl until smooth. Using a small spoon or knife, drizzle cookies with icing.

Unwrap the chilled rolls of dough and slice with a sharp knife into ½-inch-thick cookies. Place on ungreased cookie sheet.

Macadamia Nut Coconut Crisps

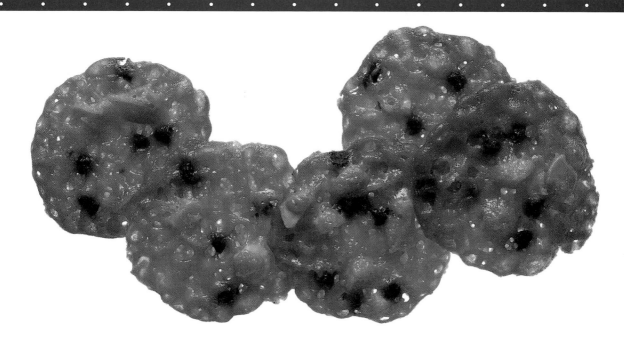

1 cup all-purpose flour
4 ounces raw macadamia nuts, coarsely
  chopped (about 1 cup)
½ cup shredded sweetened coconut
1 stick (½ cup) salted butter, softened
½ cup light corn syrup

½ cup (packed) dark brown sugar
2 teaspoons vanilla extract
2 ounces mini semisweet chocolate chips
  (about ⅓ cup)

Yield: About 3 dozen

- Preheat oven to 375°F.

- Combine flour, nuts, and coconut in a medium bowl. Set aside.

- Heat butter, corn syrup, and brown sugar in a 2-quart saucepan until boiling, stirring occasionally. Remove saucepan from heat and stir in vanilla. Add flour mixture and set aside to cool. Then add the chocolate chips and mix until all ingredients are equally distributed.

- Drop by half teaspoons onto well-greased cookie sheets, 2 inches apart. Bake for 8 to 10 minutes or until the mixture spreads and bubbles.

- Cool cookies for 1 minute on cookie sheet, then immediately transfer to a cool, flat surface with a metal spatula. Cookies will remain soft until completely cooled.

Gently spoon the dry ingredients into the heated butter-and-sugar mixture (far left). Stir after every few spoonfuls until the dry ingredients are well incorporated (left).

Maple Pecan Butter Balls

1¼ cups all-purpose flour
½ teaspoon baking soda
1 teaspoon ground cinnamon
3 ounces pecans, finely ground in food
   processor or blender (about ¾ cup)
1 stick (½ cup) salted butter, softened

⅔ cup granulated sugar
¼ cup pure maple syrup
1 large egg

Yield: About 2 dozen

- Preheat oven to 300°F.

- In a medium bowl, combine flour, soda, cinnamon, and finely ground pecans. (For extra flavor, sauté pecans in 1 tablespoon butter until slightly browned.) Mix ingredients well with a wire whisk and set aside.

- In another medium bowl, cream butter and sugar with an electric mixer set at medium speed until mixture forms a grainy paste. Add syrup and egg and beat until slightly thickened.

- Add the flour mixture and blend at low speed just until combined. Do not overmix. Place dough in a plastic bag and refrigerate until firm, about 1 hour.

- Remove dough from refrigerator and shape into 1-inch balls. Place cookies on ungreased cookie sheets, 1 inch apart. Bake for 17 to 18 minutes, or until the cookie bottoms are golden brown. Immediately transfer the cookies with a spatula to a cool, flat surface.

To make cookies more festive, sprinkle them with powdered sugar using a small mesh sieve (far left). Then, spoon chocolate icing into a pastry bag fitted with a small (#3) plain tip. Pipe decorative patterns onto cookies as shown (left).

Gingerbread Men

COOKIES
3¼ cups all-purpose flour
½ teaspoon baking soda
¼ teaspoon salt
1 teaspoon ground cinnamon
2 teaspoons ground ginger
¼ teaspoon ground cloves
2 sticks (1 cup) salted butter, softened
¾ cup (packed) dark brown sugar
1 large egg

½ cup unsulfurized molasses
3 ounces raisins (about ½ cup) (optional)

ICING
⅔ cup powdered sugar
1 to 2 teaspoons milk

Yield: About 2½ dozen 6-inch cookies
About 3½ dozen 4-inch cookies

- Preheat oven to 325°F.

- Combine flour, soda, salt, cinnamon, ginger, and cloves in a medium bowl.

- In a large bowl with an electric mixer cream butter and sugar. Scrape down the sides of the bowl. Add egg and molasses, and beat on medium speed until smooth. Scrape bowl and add the flour mixture. Blend on low speed just until combined; do not overmix.

- Separate dough into 2 balls and flatten into disks. Wrap each disk tightly in plastic wrap or a plastic bag, and refrigerate 1 hour or until firm.

- On floured surface with floured rolling pin, roll dough out to ¼-inch thickness. With floured cookie

cutters, cut into gingerbread men. Gather scraps and reroll dough until all dough is used. Place on ungreased cookie sheets ½ inch apart.

- If you want to use raisins to decorate the cookies, plump raisins first by soaking them in warm water for 5 minutes. Discard water. Use raisins as eyes, mouths, and buttons.

- Bake for 9 to 11 minutes being careful not to brown. Transfer to a cool, flat surface with a spatula.

- Prepare the icing: Whisk sugar and milk together in a small bowl until mixture is smooth but liquid. If it seems dry, add ¼ teaspoon more milk. Spoon icing into a pastry bag fitted with a small piping tip. Decorate gingerbread men as desired.

Christmas Sugar Cookies

2 cups all-purpose flour
¼ teaspoon salt
1½ sticks (¾ cup) salted butter, softened
¾ cup granulated sugar
1 large egg

1 teaspoon vanilla extract
Colored sugars or sprinkles

Yield: About 3 dozen

- Preheat oven to 325°F.

- In a medium bowl, combine the flour and salt with a wire whisk.

- In a large bowl, cream the butter and sugar with an electric mixer on medium speed. Add the egg and vanilla, and beat until well mixed. Scrape down sides of bowl, then add the flour mixture. Blend on low speed just until combined. Do not overmix.

- Gather dough into a ball. Flatten the ball into a

disk and wrap tightly in plastic wrap or a plastic bag. Refrigerate 1 hour or until firm.

- On a floured surface, roll out dough to a ¼-inch thickness. With cookie cutters, cut dough into desired shapes and place on ungreased cookie sheets. Decorate with colored sugars or sprinkles.

- Bake for 13 to 15 minutes, being careful not to brown. Immediately transfer cookies with a spatula to a cool, flat surface.

Brown Sugar Shortbread

SHORTBREAD

2 sticks (1 cup) salted butter, softened
¾ cup (packed) light brown sugar
2 teaspoons vanilla extract
2 cups all-purpose flour

TOPPING

1 tablespoon salted butter
6 ounces semisweet chocolate chips
  (about 1 cup)
4 ounces pecans, finely chopped
  (about 1 cup)

Yield: About 2½ dozen

- Preheat oven to 325°F.

- In a large bowl, cream butter and sugar with an electric mixer at medium speed. Scrape down sides of bowl. Then add vanilla and flour, and blend thoroughly on low speed.

- Shape level tablespoons of dough into 1-inch balls, then form into logs 2 inches long and 1 inch wide. Place on ungreased cookie sheets, 2 inches apart.

- Bake for 17 to 19 minutes, or until cookies spread, and turn a light golden brown. Transfer to a cool, flat surface.

- Make topping: Melt butter and chocolate chips in a double boiler over hot, not boiling, water, or in a microwave oven on high power. Stir chocolate every 30 seconds until melted.

- Dip top of each cooled shortbread cookie into melted chocolate, then into chopped pecans. Place cookies on wax paper and refrigerate to set.

Floating Heaven

BUTTER COOKIES
1 stick (½ cup) unsalted butter, softened
⅔ cup granulated sugar
2 large eggs
1 teaspoon vanilla extract
1 cup plus 2 tablespoons all-purpose flour

DARK CHOCOLATE MOUSSE
5 ounces semisweet chocolate, finely chopped
1 cup plus 2 tablespoons heavy cream
1 tablespoon powdered sugar
½ teaspoon vanilla extract

CARAMEL CRÈME ANGLAISE
¾ cup granulated sugar
¼ cup water
2½ cups light cream, scalded
4 large egg yolks
1 stick (½ cup) unsalted butter, softened
2 teaspoons vanilla extract
Unsweetened cocoa powder, for garnish

Yield: About 12 servings

- Make the cookies: In a medium bowl, cream the butter and sugar. Beat in the eggs and vanilla. Blend in the flour. Chill the dough for 1 hour.

- Preheat the oven to 325°F. Roll the dough into 24 balls and place 2 inches apart on ungreased cookie sheets. Flatten the cookies with the bottom of a glass and bake for 14 to 16 minutes, or until the edges turn golden. Transfer to racks to cool.

- Meanwhile, make the mousse: Place the chocolate in a medium bowl. In a small, heavy saucepan, bring ½ cup of the cream to a boil. Pour the hot cream over the chocolate and let stand, covered, for 5 minutes, then stir until smooth. Transfer the chocolate cream to a medium bowl.

- In another medium bowl, beat the remaining ½ cup plus 2 tablespoons cream with the powdered sugar and vanilla until soft peaks form. Fold ⅓ of the whipped cream into the chocolate cream to lighten it. Gently but thoroughly fold in the remaining whipped cream. Refrigerate until firm.

- Make the crème anglaise: In a heavy, medium saucepan, dissolve the granulated sugar in the water over low heat, stirring constantly. Increase the heat to medium-high and boil without stirring until the syrup turns a deep amber. Remove the pan from the heat and stir in the hot cream (be careful, it will bubble rapidly). Stir until smooth.

- In a small bowl, whisk the egg yolks. Slowly beat in 1 cup of the hot caramel sauce to warm the egg yolks. Transfer the warmed egg yolks to the pan and cook over medium heat, stirring constantly, until the crème anglaise lightly coats the back of a spoon. Do not boil. Strain the sauce through a fine-mesh sieve and stir in the butter and vanilla. Keep warm.

- Assemble: With a pastry bag fitted with a star tip, pipe rosettes of mousse over a cookie and top with a second cookie; decorate the top with cocoa powder dusted through a heart-shaped stencil. Spoon ¼ cup of the warm crème anglaise onto a small plate and place a floating heaven on top.

Chocolate-Glazed Shortbread Cookies

SHORTBREAD
3 sticks (1½ cups) salted butter, softened
1 cup powdered sugar
1 tablespoon vanilla extract
3 cups all-purpose flour

CHOCOLATE GLAZE
¼ cup heavy cream
6 ounces semisweet chocolate chips
  (about 1 cup)
2 teaspoons light corn syrup

Yield: About 4 dozen

- Preheat oven to 325°F.

- Blend butter until smooth in a large bowl using an electric mixer set at medium speed. Slowly blend in the powdered sugar. Scrape down the sides of the bowl, then add vanilla extract and combine thoroughly. Add flour and mix at low speed until well blended.

- Divide dough into 2 roughly equal pieces. Flatten each piece into a disk and wrap in plastic wrap. Refrigerate disks until firm, about 1½ hours.

- On a floured board using a floured rolling pin, roll out disks to ⅛-inch thickness. Turn dough often to prevent sticking. Cut cookies with flour-dipped cookie cutters. Bake on ungreased cookie sheets for 16 to 18 minutes, being careful not to let the cookies brown. Transfer cookies at once to a cool, flat surface with a spatula.

- Prepare the chocolate glaze: Heat cream in a small saucepan until scalded; remove from heat. Stir in chocolate chips and corn syrup, cover, and let stand for 15 minutes. With small wire whisk or wooden spoon gently mix glaze until smooth, being careful not to create bubbles in the chocolate. Dip all or half of each cookie into glaze and transfer to a tray or cool cookie sheet covered with wax paper. Chill cookies in refrigerator for 10 minutes to set.

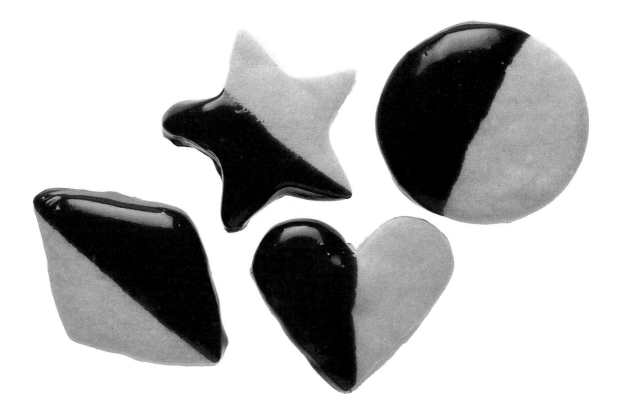

Bizcochitos

COOKIES
2¾ cups all-purpose flour
½ teaspoon baking soda
¼ teaspoon salt
2½ teaspoons aniseed
¾ cup (packed) light brown sugar
¾ cup granulated sugar
2 sticks (1 cup) salted butter, softened

2 large eggs
2 teaspoons brandy

TOPPING
¼ cup granulated sugar
2 tablespoons ground cinnamon

Yield: About 3 dozen

- Preheat oven to 300°F.

- Combine flour, baking soda, salt, and aniseed in a small bowl and set aside.

- Blend sugars in a medium bowl using an electric mixer set at medium speed. Add butter and mix until grainy, scraping down the sides of the bowl. Add eggs and brandy, and beat at medium speed until light and fluffy.

- Add the flour mixture and mix at low speed until just combined. Do not overmix.

- Roll rounded tablespoons of dough into 1-inch-diameter balls and then flatten each one slightly with the bottom of a glass or a spatula. Press tops into sugar-cinnamon mixture, then place them on ungreased cookie sheets, 1½ inches apart. Bake for 22 to 24 minutes until cookies are slightly brown along edges.

- Transfer cookies immediately to a cool surface with a spatula.

Cinnamon Sugar Butter Cookies

TOPPING
3 tablespoons granulated sugar
1 tablespoon ground cinnamon

COOKIES
2½ cups all-purpose flour
½ teaspoon baking soda
¼ teaspoon salt

1 cup (packed) dark brown sugar
½ cup granulated sugar
2 sticks (1 cup) salted butter, softened
2 large eggs
2 teaspoons vanilla extract

Yield: About 3 dozen

- Preheat oven to 300°F.

- In a small bowl, combine sugar and cinnamon for topping. Set aside.

- In a medium bowl, combine flour, soda, and salt. Mix well with a wire whisk and set aside.

- In a large bowl blend sugars with an electric mixer set at medium speed. Add the butter and mix to form a grainy paste. Scrape sides of bowl, then add the eggs and vanilla. Mix at medium speed until light and fluffy.

- Add the flour mixture and blend at low speed just until combined. Do not overmix. Shape dough into 1-inch balls and roll each ball in cinnamon-sugar topping.

- Place onto ungreased cookie sheets, 2 inches apart. Bake for 18 to 20 minutes. Immediately transfer cookies with a spatula to a cool, flat surface.

Gingersnaps

2½ cups all-purpose flour
½ teaspoon baking soda
¼ teaspoon salt
2 teaspoons ground ginger
1 teaspoon diced crystallized ginger
½ teaspoon allspice
½ teaspoon ground black pepper

1¼ cups (packed) dark brown sugar
1½ sticks (¾ cup) salted butter, softened
1 large egg
¼ cup unsulfurized molasses

Yield: About 2½ dozen

- Preheat oven to 300°F.

- In a medium bowl, combine flour, soda, salt, ground ginger, crystallized ginger, allspice, and pepper. Mix well with a wire whisk. Set aside.

- In a large bowl, mix sugar and butter with an electric mixer set at medium speed. Scrape down the sides of the bowl. Add egg and molasses, and beat at medium speed until light and fluffy.

- Add the flour mixture and mix at low speed just until combined. Do not overmix. Chill the dough in the refrigerator for 1 hour—the dough will be less sticky and easier to handle.

- Form dough into balls 1 inch in diameter. Place onto ungreased cookie sheets, 1½ inches apart. Bake for 24 to 25 minutes. Use a spatula to immediately transfer cookies to a cool, flat surface.

Apple Cobbler Cookies

COOKIES

3 cups all-purpose flour
1 teaspoon baking powder
1 teaspoon ground cinnamon
½ cup granulated sugar
½ cup (packed) light brown sugar
2 sticks (1 cup) salted butter, softened
2 large eggs
2 teaspoons vanilla extract
¼ cup apple juice
½ cup apple butter
1 cup tart apples, peeled and chopped

6 ounces raisins (about 1 cup)
4 ounces pecans, finely chopped
 (about 1 cup)

CRUMB COATING

1¼ cups (packed) light brown sugar
1½ cups quick oats (not instant)
1¼ teaspoons ground cinnamon
9 tablespoons salted butter, melted

Yield: About 4 dozen

• Preheat oven to 300°F.

• In a medium bowl, combine flour, baking powder, and cinnamon. Mix well with wire whisk. Set aside.

• Combine sugars in a large bowl. Add butter and mix using an electric mixer set at medium speed, scraping down the sides of the bowl. Add eggs and vanilla, and blend until smooth. Thoroughly incorporate the apple juice and apple butter. Add the flour mixture, chopped apples, raisins, and pecans, and blend at low speed until just combined. Do not overmix.

• Prepare the crumb coating: Combine sugar, oats, and cinnamon in a medium bowl. Mix well with a wire whisk. Add melted butter and mix until dry ingredients are well moistened. Set aside.

• Roll dough into 1-inch-diameter balls. Roll each ball in crumb mixture until well coated. Place cookies on ungreased cookie sheets, 2 inches apart. Bake for 24 to 26 minutes, or until cookie is firm to the touch and crumb coating begins to brown. Transfer to a cool, flat surface.

Roll each ball of dough in the crumb coating until it is completely covered. It may be necessary to press the mixture into the dough to make sure it sticks. Place the coated balls on ungreased cookie sheets and bake as directed.

Russian Tea Cakes

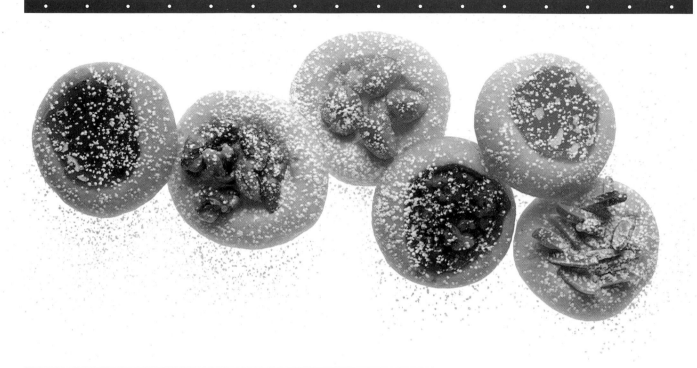

COOKIES

2 sticks (1 cup) salted butter, softened
½ cup powdered sugar
2 teaspoons vanilla extract
2 cups all-purpose flour
¼ teaspoon salt

TOPPING

½ cup fruit preserves or
2 ounces chopped walnuts (about ½ cup)
¼ cup powdered sugar

Yield: About 2 dozen

- Preheat oven to 325°F.

- In a large bowl, cream butter and sugar using an electric mixer. Add vanilla, scraping down sides of bowl as needed. Blend in flour and salt, mixing until thoroughly combined.

- Roll tablespoons of dough into small balls about 1 inch in diameter. Place dough balls on lightly greased cookie sheets about 1 inch apart. Press down the center of each ball with a spoon, forming a depression. Fill each with a teaspoon of preserves or nuts.

- Bake for 15 to 20 minutes or until golden brown. Transfer cookies immediately to a cool, flat surface. When cookies are completely cool, dust them lightly with powdered sugar.

Brown Buttercrunch Cookies

COOKIES
1 stick (½ cup) salted butter, softened
½ cup corn syrup
⅔ cup (packed) dark brown sugar
1 cup old-fashioned oats
  (not quick or instant)
¾ cup all-purpose flour
1 teaspoon vanilla extract

CHOCOLATE GLAZE
¼ cup heavy cream
6 ounces semisweet chocolate chips
  (about 1 cup)
2 teaspoons light corn syrup

Yield: About 2½ dozen

- Preheat oven to 375°F. Line cookie sheets with parchment paper.

- In a medium saucepan, melt butter, corn syrup, and brown sugar over moderate heat, stirring constantly until sugar dissolves. Increase heat to high. When mixture boils remove from heat and stir in oats, flour, and vanilla.

- Bake cookies 1 sheet at a time and be ready to work fast. Drop by half teaspoons 3 inches apart onto paper-lined cookie sheets. Bake for 8 minutes or until mixture spreads, bubbles, and begins to brown. Let cookies cool for 1 to 2 minutes before rolling.

- Roll widest edge of cookie around a pencil or wooden spoon handle, creating a tube. Repeat with remaining cookies. If cookies become too brittle to roll, return to oven for about 30 seconds to soften. Cool rolled cookies completely.

- Make the chocolate glaze: Heat cream in a small saucepan until scalded. Remove from heat and stir in chocolate chips and corn syrup. Cover and let stand about 15 minutes until chocolate has melted. Using a wire whisk or wooden spoon, gently mix the glaze until it is smooth, being careful not to create bubbles.

- When cookies are cool, dip all or half of each cookie into the glaze and return to parchment paper. Refrigerate for 10 to 15 minutes to set.

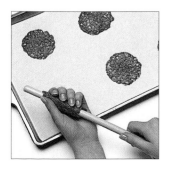

Wrap the warm cookie around a wooden spoon handle (far left). If cookie cools too much, it may crack when rolled. Dip half of each rolled cookie in melted chocolate and return to cookie sheet (left).

Sweetie Pies

2 ounces unsweetened chocolate
4 ounces semisweet chocolate chips
  (about ¾ cup)
1 stick (½ cup) salted butter, softened
1 cup granulated sugar
2 large eggs
2 teaspoons vanilla extract
1½ cups all-purpose flour

6 ounces semisweet chocolate chips
  (about 1 cup)
3 ounces white chocolate chips
  (about ½ cup)
1½ ounces milk chocolate chips
  (about ¼ cup)

Yield: About 2½ dozen

- Preheat oven to 375°F. Line cookie sheets with wax paper.

- In a double boiler, melt the unsweetened chocolate and the first batch of chocolate chips. Stir frequently with wooden spoon or wire whisk until creamy and smooth.

- Pour melted chocolate into a large bowl. Add butter and beat with electric mixer at medium speed until thoroughly combined.

- Add the sugar, eggs, and vanilla. Beat on medium speed until well blended. Scrape down sides of the bowl.

- Add the flour and the 3 types of chocolate chips. Mix at low speed just until combined. Chips should be distributed equally throughout the dough.

- Roll a heaping tablespoon of dough into a ball, about 1½ inches in diameter. Place dough balls onto paper-lined sheets, 2 inches apart. With the palm of your hand, flatten each ball to ½-inch thickness.

- Bake for 10 to 12 minutes. Transfer cookies with a spatula to a cool, flat surface.

Choconut Macaroons

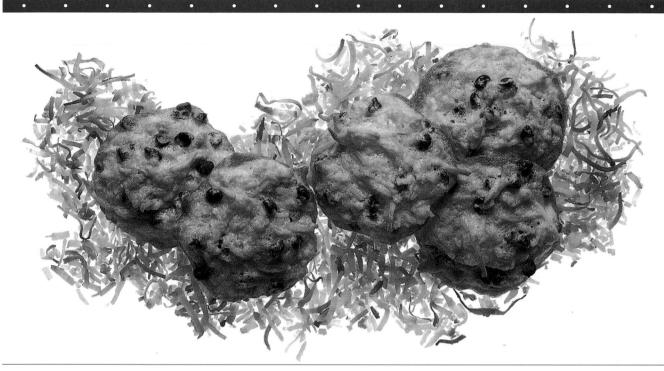

¼ cup granulated sugar
2 tablespoons almond paste (marzipan)
1 cup shredded sweetened coconut
2 ounces mini semisweet chocolate chips
  (about ⅓ cup)

3 large egg whites
½ teaspoon cream of tartar

Yield: About 1½ dozen

- Preheat oven to 325°F.

- Combine almond paste and sugar in a medium bowl. Using your fingers, work paste into sugar completely. Add coconut and chocolate chips and stir to combine.

- In another medium bowl, beat egg whites until fluffy using absolutely clean beaters. Add cream of tartar and beat on high until stiff peaks form. Add half of beaten egg whites to coconut mixture and combine to lighten. Fold in remaining whites gently, being careful not to deflate.

- Drop by rounded teaspoons onto lightly greased cookie sheets. Bake for 20 minutes, or until tops are lightly browned. Cool 1 minute on the cookie sheets before transferring cookies to a cool surface.

Spoon about half of the beaten egg whites into the cookie batter, and stir lightly but thoroughly until the egg whites are well combined (far left). Add the remaining egg whites and, using a spatula, bring the lightened batter up from the bottom of the bowl over the egg whites (left). Continue folding the egg whites into the batter just until they are incorporated. Be careful not to deflate the egg whites.

Cinnamon Maple Rings

PASTRY
2 cups all-purpose flour
¼ cup granulated sugar
2 sticks (1 cup) salted butter, chilled & sliced
  into 8 pieces
¼ cup pure maple syrup, chilled
2 to 4 tablespoons ice water

FILLING
¼ cup granulated sugar
4 teaspoons ground cinnamon

TOPPING
¼ cup pure maple syrup

Yield: About 4 dozen

- Combine flour and sugar in a medium bowl using an electric mixer set on medium speed. Add butter and mix until the dough forms pea-size pellets. Add chilled maple syrup and 2 tablespoons of water, and mix on low speed until dough can be formed into a ball. Do not overmix, or the pastry will be tough.

- Separate dough into 2 balls and flatten into disks. Wrap dough tightly in plastic wrap or place in plastic bags. Refrigerate for 2 hours or until firm.

- Prepare the filling: Combine sugar and cinnamon in a small bowl. Preheat oven to 325°F.

- Using a floured rolling pin on a floured board, roll one piece of dough into a rough rectangle 10 inches wide, 15 inches long, and ⅛ inch thick. Sprinkle

After sprinkling the dough with the cinnamon-sugar filling, roll the dough into a tight cylinder (right). Just before sliding the cookies into the oven, brush the tops with maple syrup (far right).

dough with half of cinnamon-sugar filling. Starting with smaller side, roll dough up tightly into a cylinder. Dampen edge with water and seal. Repeat with remaining dough. Wrap each roll in plastic wrap and refrigerate for 1 hour.

- Using a sharp, thin knife, cut ¼-inch slices from each roll. Place slices on ungreased cookie sheets, 1 inch apart. Brush tops lightly with ¼ cup maple syrup. Bake for 16 to 17 minutes, or until light golden brown. Immediately transfer cookies to a cool, flat surface with a spatula.

Party Time Cookies

1½ sticks (¾ cup) salted butter, softened
⅓ cup granulated sugar
1 teaspoon vanilla extract
¼ teaspoon almond extract
1 cup all-purpose flour

6 ounces semisweet chocolate chips
  (about 1 cup)
4 ounces slivered almonds (about 1 cup)

Yield: About 2 dozen

- Preheat oven to 350°F.

- Cream butter and sugar together in a medium bowl using an electric mixer set at medium speed. Add extracts and beat well. Scrape bowl. Add flour, chocolate chips, and almonds, and blend on low speed until just combined. Do not overmix.

- Shape rounded tablespoons into 1½-inch balls and place on ungreased cookie sheets, 2 inches apart. Press balls with palm of hand or bottom of drinking glass into ½-inch-thick rounds.

- Bake for 15 to 17 minutes or until cookies just begin to brown. Transfer cookies to a cool, flat surface.

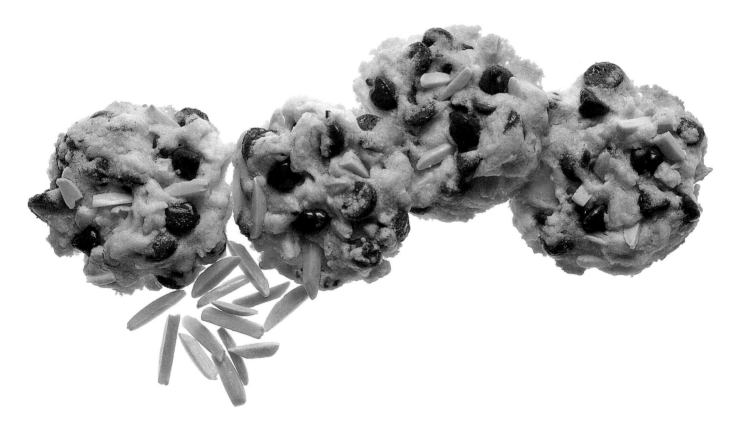

Snowy White Chocolate Crescents

1½ cups all-purpose flour
⅓ cup cocoa powder, unsweetened
1 stick (½ cup) salted butter, softened
1 cup granulated sugar
1 teaspoon vanilla extract

1 large egg
½ cup powdered sugar

Yield: About 2½ dozen

- Preheat oven to 325°F.

- In a small bowl, combine flour and cocoa. Mix well with a wire whisk and set aside.

- In a medium bowl, cream butter and sugar with an electric mixer on medium speed. Add vanilla and egg, and beat until light and smooth. Scrape down sides of bowl, then add flour and cocoa mixture. Blend on low speed until fully incorporated. The dough will be dry and crumbly.

- Shape a level tablespoon of dough into a 3½-inch log. Slightly bend the log to form a crescent shape. Form remaining dough into crescents, and place on ungreased cookie sheets, 1 inch apart. Bake for 15 to 17 minutes or until the outside of cookie is hard but the center remains soft.

- Cool on cookie sheets for 2 to 3 minutes, then transfer to a flat surface to cool a few minutes more. While still warm, roll the cookies in powdered sugar until coated.

To form the chocolate cookies, roll dough briskly between your hands into 3½-inch logs (far left). Then bend each log slightly to form a crescent shape (left) and bake.

Double-Dipped Chocolate Shortbread Cookies

COOKIES

3 ounces semisweet chocolate, finely chopped
1½ sticks (¾ cup) unsalted butter, softened
1 teaspoon vanilla extract
1½ cups all-purpose flour
½ cup powdered sugar
2 teaspoons unsweetened cocoa powder
⅛ teaspoon salt

FOR DIPPING

4 ounces white chocolate, finely chopped
½ cup heavy cream
3 ounces semisweet chocolate, finely chopped

Yield: About 2½ dozen

● Make the cookies: In a double boiler, melt the semisweet chocolate over hot, not simmering, water. Set aside to cool to lukewarm.

● In a large bowl with an electric mixer, cream the butter. Beat in the melted chocolate. Then beat in the vanilla, flour, sugar, cocoa, and salt. Wrap and chill the dough for 30 minutes, or until firm enough to roll into balls.

● Preheat the oven to 350°F. Roll the dough into 1-inch balls, then roll each ball into a thick log. Place on an ungreased cookie sheet and press the dough to a ¼-inch thickness with the tines of a fork, keeping the cookies oval in shape.

● Bake the cookies for 8 to 10 minutes, or until just set; do not overbake. Transfer to wire racks to cool completely.

● Dip the cookies: In a small bowl set over a saucepan of hot water, melt the white chocolate with ¼ cup of the cream; stir until smooth. Keep the mixture over the hot water so it will be liquid for dipping. In another small bowl set over a saucepan of hot water, melt the semisweet chocolate with the remaining ¼ cup cream; stir until smooth. Keep warm.

● Dip one end of a cookie in the white chocolate and the other end in the dark chocolate and return to the cooling racks so the chocolate can set. Repeat with the remaining cookies.

Chocolate Meringue Puffs

2 ounces unsweetened baking chocolate square
¾ cup powdered sugar, sifted
3 tablespoons unsweetened cocoa
   powder, sifted
3 large egg whites

½ teaspoon cream of tartar
½ cup granulated sugar

Yield: About 2½ dozen

- Line cookie sheets with foil.

- Finely chop baking chocolate square in a blender, and set aside.

- In a small bowl combine powdered sugar and cocoa with a wire whisk.

- In a medium bowl beat egg whites and cream of tartar with an electric mixer at medium speed until mixture thickens. Increase speed to high, while adding the granulated sugar slowly. Beat until mixture forms stiff peaks and turns glossy.

- Gently fold in cocoa mixture and chopped baking chocolate with a rubber spatula. Fold ingredients into egg whites until mixture is uniformly brown with no streaks.

- Fill a pastry bag fitted with a large star tip with the meringue. Pipe meringue in decorative shapes onto foil-lined cookie sheets.

- Preheat oven to 200° F.

- Allow meringues to dry at room temperature for about 45 minutes or until not sticky. (Don't try making these on humid or rainy days.) Bake for 1 hour. When cool, remove from foil with a metal spatula.

Spoon the meringue into a pastry bag with a large star tip. Pipe meringue in decorative shapes onto foil-lined cookie sheets. If you don't have a pastry bag, drop the meringue by tablespoonfuls onto the foil.

Bar Cookies

Chocolate Chip Butterscotch Bars

2 cups all-purpose flour
½ teaspoon baking soda
1 cup (packed) dark brown sugar
2 sticks (1 cup) salted butter, softened
1 large egg
2 teaspoons vanilla extract

4 ounces chopped pecans (about 1 cup)
9 ounces semisweet chocolate chips
  (about 1½ cups)

Yield: 16 bars

- Preheat oven to 300°F. Grease an 8-by-8-inch baking pan.

- Combine flour and soda in a medium bowl. Mix well with a wire whisk. Set aside.

- In a large bowl, use an electric mixer to blend the sugar and butter. Add egg and vanilla, and beat at medium speed until light and smooth. Scrape down the sides of the bowl, then add the flour mixture, pecans, and chocolate chips. Blend at low speed until just combined. Do not overmix.

- Transfer batter into the prepared pan, and level top with a rubber spatula. Bake in center of oven for 35 to 45 minutes or until toothpick comes out clean but center is still soft. Cool on rack to room temperature. Cut with sharp knife into 1-by-2-inch bars.

Peanut Butter & Jelly Squares

2½ cups all-purpose flour
½ teaspoon baking powder
2 sticks (1 cup) salted butter, softened
1 cup granulated sugar
1 large egg
2 teaspoons vanilla extract

½ cup jam or jelly
¼ cup creamy peanut butter
2 tablespoons powdered sugar

Yield: 24 squares

- Preheat oven to 325°F. Lightly grease a 9-by-13-inch baking pan.

- In a medium bowl, combine flour and baking powder. Mix well with a wire whisk and set aside.

- In another medium bowl with an electric mixer on medium speed, combine butter and sugar to form a grainy paste. Add egg and vanilla, and mix until smooth. Scrape down sides of bowl. Then add flour mixture and blend at low speed until thoroughly combined. Dough will be firm.

- Divide dough into 2 pieces; form disks and wrap tightly in plastic wrap or a plastic bag. Refrigerate for 1 hour.

- On floured board using a floured rolling pin, roll out each disk to 9 by 13 inches, about ¼ inch thick. Place 1 piece in bottom and up the sides of prepared baking pan. Refrigerate 10 minutes more.

- Spread half the jelly on dough. Layer peanut butter on top of jelly, then top with remaining jelly. Sprinkle with powdered sugar. Place second dough rectangle on top of peanut-butter-and-jelly layer. Pinch down side edges all around inside of pan.

- Bake for 35 to 40 minutes or until golden brown and firm to the touch in the center. Cool in pan, then cut into squares.

Golden White-Chunk Nutty Bars

2 cups all-purpose flour
½ teaspoon baking soda
¼ teaspoon salt
1½ sticks (¾ cup) unsalted butter, cut into
  tablespoons
1 cup (packed) dark brown sugar
2 large eggs

½ cup shredded coconut
2 teaspoons vanilla extract
10 ounces white chocolate, coarsely chopped
1 cup coarsely chopped pecans

Yield: 16 bars

- Preheat the oven to 300°F. Grease a 9-by-13-inch baking pan.

- In a medium bowl, combine the flour, baking soda, and salt.

- In another medium bowl with an electric mixer, cream the butter and sugar. Beat in the eggs, coconut, and vanilla, then blend slowly until smooth. Add the flour mixture, chopped chocolate, and pecans.

- Scrape the dough into the prepared baking pan and level and smooth the surface. Bake for 40 to 45 minutes, or until the center is set and the top is golden.

- Place the pan on a wire rack to cool to room temperature before cutting into 16 bars.

Cherry Cream Bars

BROWNIE LAYER

1 cup all-purpose flour
1 cup granulated sugar
¾ cup (packed) dark brown sugar
½ teaspoon salt
4 ounces unsweetened chocolate
1½ sticks (¾ cup) unsalted butter, softened
4 large eggs
¼ cup milk
2½ teaspoons vanilla extract
1 cup coarsely chopped walnuts
1 cup drained canned Bing cherries (½ cup of
  the syrup reserved)
1 cup semisweet chocolate chips

CHOCOLATE-CHERRY GLAZE

3 ounces semisweet chocolate, chopped
½ cup syrup reserved from cherries
¼ cup heavy cream
2 teaspoons kirsch (cherry brandy)
2 teaspoons granulated sugar

CHERRY CREAM

1 cup heavy cream
3 tablespoons powdered sugar
1 tablespoon kirsch (cherry brandy)
½ cup chopped drained canned
  Bing cherries

Yield: 12 bars

• Preheat the oven to 300°F. Grease a 7-by-11-inch baking pan.

• Make the brownie layer: In a large bowl, whisk together the flour, granulated sugar, brown sugar, and salt.

• In a double boiler, melt the unsweetened chocolate and butter together over low heat, stirring until smooth.

• In a small bowl, lightly beat the eggs with the milk and vanilla.

• Add the chocolate mixture and beaten eggs to the dry ingredients and stir to blend. Stir in the walnuts, cherries, and chocolate chips.

• Pour the batter into the prepared pan and bake for 1 hour and 10 minutes, or until a cake tester inserted in the center comes out with a few crumbs clinging to it. Cool the brownies in the pan on a rack.

• Meanwhile, make the chocolate-cherry glaze: Place the semisweet chocolate in a medium bowl.

• In a small saucepan, bring the reserved cherry syrup to a boil. Simmer until reduced by half. Add the cream and bring to a boil. Remove from the heat and stir in the kirsch and granulated sugar.

• Pour the hot cream mixture over the chocolate. Let stand, covered, for 5 minutes, then stir until smooth. Set aside to cool to room temperature, then pour the glaze over the cooled brownies.

• Make the cherry cream: In a medium bowl, beat the cream with the powdered sugar and kirsch until stiff peaks form. Fold in the drained chopped cherries.

• Cut into 12 bars and serve with a spoonful of the cherry cream on top.

Bull's Eyes

BLUE-RIBBON CHOCOLATE CHIP COOKIES
2½ cups all-purpose flour
½ teaspoon baking soda
¼ teaspoon salt
1 cup (packed) dark brown sugar
½ cup granulated sugar
2 sticks (1 cup) salted butter, softened
2 large eggs
2 teaspoons vanilla extract
12 ounces semisweet chocolate chips
  (about 2 cups)
1 cup sweetened, shredded coconut

DOUBLE-RICH CHOCOLATE COOKIES
1¼ cups all-purpose flour
¼ teaspoon baking soda
⅛ teaspoon salt
¼ cup unsweetened cocoa powder
½ cup (packed) dark brown sugar
¼ cup plus 2 tablespoons granulated sugar
1 stick (½ cup) salted butter, softened
1 large egg
1 large egg yolk
1 teaspoon vanilla extract
6 ounces semisweet chocolate chips
  (about 1 cup)

Yield: 24 bars

- Preheat oven to 300°F and grease a 9-by-13-inch glass baking dish.

- First, make the Blue-Ribbon Cookies: In a medium bowl combine flour, soda, and salt. Mix well.

- In a large bowl, blend sugars and butter with an electric mixer. Scrape sides of bowl, then add eggs and vanilla extract. Beat at medium speed until light and fluffy. Add flour mixture and chocolate chips, and mix just until combined. Press dough evenly into prepared pan and sprinkle with coconut. Set aside.

- Next, make the Double-Rich Cookies: In a medium bowl combine flour, soda, salt, and cocoa powder with a wire whisk.

- In a large bowl, blend sugars and butter with mixer at medium speed. Scrape bowl, then add eggs and vanilla, and beat until well combined. Add the flour mixture and chocolate chips, and blend on low. Do not overmix.

- Drop the Double-Rich dough by rounded teaspoons onto the Blue-Ribbon dough. Evenly space the darker dough on top of the lighter dough to resemble bull's eyes. Bake 50 to 60 minutes, until a toothpick inserted in center comes out clean. Cool and cut.

Creamy Layered Pudding Bars

CRUST

1 stick (½ cup) salted butter, softened
¼ cup granulated sugar
1 large egg yolk
1 teaspoon vanilla extract
1 cup cake flour
⅛ teaspoon salt

FILLING

½ cup granulated sugar
1 tablespoon cornstarch
5 large egg yolks
1 teaspoon vanilla extract
1 cup whipping cream
6 ounces mini semisweet chocolate chips
  (about 1 cup)
4 ounces pecans, chopped (about 1 cup)

Yield: 16 bars

- Preheat oven to 325°F. Grease an 8-by-8-inch baking pan.

- In a medium bowl, cream the butter and sugar with an electric mixer at medium speed, scraping down the sides of the bowl. Add single egg yolk and vanilla and beat at medium speed until light and fluffy. Add the flour and the salt, and blend at low speed until just combined.

- Turn dough out into prepared pan, and place in refrigerator for 15 minutes. When dough is chilled, lightly flour your hands and press the dough to ¼-inch thickness on bottom and sides of pan. Dough should extend 1 inch up sides of pan. Return pan to refrigerator while you prepare the filling.

- Prepare the filling: Combine sugar and cornstarch in a small bowl. Mix well with a wire whisk. Set aside.

- In a medium bowl with an electric mixer set on medium-high speed, beat the 5 egg yolks

5 minutes or until they are light and fluffy. Add cornstarch-sugar mixture and mix on medium until combined. Add the vanilla, whipping cream, chocolate chips, and pecans and blend at low speed—scraping bowl as needed—until thoroughly combined. Pour filling into pastry-lined pan.

- Bake for 55 to 60 minutes or until filling is set and golden brown. Chill 4 hours or overnight. Cut into 16 bars.

Press the chilled dough firmly into the bottom of a greased 8-by-8-inch pan. The dough should extend up the sides of the pan by about an inch. Lightly flour your hands before you begin to prevent the dough from sticking to them.

Pecan Pie Bars

PASTRY

1½ cups all-purpose flour
1 stick (½ cup) salted butter, chilled
5 to 6 tablespoons ice water

FILLING

5 tablespoons salted butter
1 cup (packed) dark brown sugar

½ cup light corn syrup
2 teaspoons vanilla extract
3 large eggs, beaten
6 ounces chopped pecans (about 1½ cups)
16 pecan halves

Yield: 16 bars

- Preheat oven to 350°F.

- In a medium bowl, combine flour and chilled butter with a pastry cutter until dough resembles coarse meal. Add water gradually and mix just until dough holds together and can be shaped into a ball. Or, use a food processor fitted with metal blade to combine flour and butter until they resemble coarse meal. Add water by tablespoonfuls and process just until a dough ball begins to form. Wrap dough tightly in plastic wrap or a plastic bag. Refrigerate for 1 hour or until firm.

- On floured board using a floured rolling pin, roll out dough into a 10-inch square. Fold dough in half and then into quarters. Place it in an 8-by-8-

inch baking pan. Unfold the dough and press it into the corners and up along the sides of the pan. Refrigerate for 15 minutes.

- Prepare the filling: Melt 5 tablespoons of butter in a medium saucepan over medium heat. Remove from heat, and stir in sugar and corn syrup. Mix until smooth. Add vanilla and eggs, and beat with spoon until thoroughly combined. Fold in chopped pecans.

- Pour the pecan filling into the pastry-lined pan. If dough extends beyond filling mixture trim dough with a knife. Place pan in center of oven and bake 50 to 60 minutes or until filling is set. Cool on wire rack. Cut into 2-inch squares, and top each with a pecan half. Serve at room temperature or chilled.

To transfer the dough from the work surface to the pan, first fold it into quarters. Place the dough in the baking pan (far left), then unfold it. Press the dough into the bottom, corners, and up the sides of the pan (left). Refrigerate for 15 minutes while you prepare the filling.

Kandy Fun Kakes

½ stick (¼ cup) unsalted butter
4 cups mini marshmallows
2 teaspoons vanilla extract
4 cups crisp rice cereal
¾ cup butterscotch caramel fudge topping

12 ounces milk chocolate,
  coarsely chopped

Yield: 16 squares

- Lightly grease a 7-by-11-inch or an 8-by-8 inch baking pan.

- In a large saucepan, melt the butter over low heat. Add the marshmallows and stir until blended. Remove from the heat and stir in the vanilla.

- Stir in the cereal and mix with a wooden spoon until thoroughly blended. Scrape the mixture into the prepared pan. With lightly buttered hands or a lightly buttered spatula, press gently on the mixture to level. Place in the freezer for 10 minutes.

- In a small saucepan, warm the butterscotch caramel fudge topping to lukewarm (do not let it get hot). Remove from the heat and set aside to cool slightly.

- Pour the warm butterscotch topping over the cereal layer, spreading evenly. Place in the freezer for 10 minutes.

- In a double boiler, melt the chocolate over hot, not simmering, water. Set aside to cool slightly. Spread the chocolate on top of the caramel mixture. Chill to set the chocolate. Cut into squares and serve.

Triple-Layered Lemon Bars

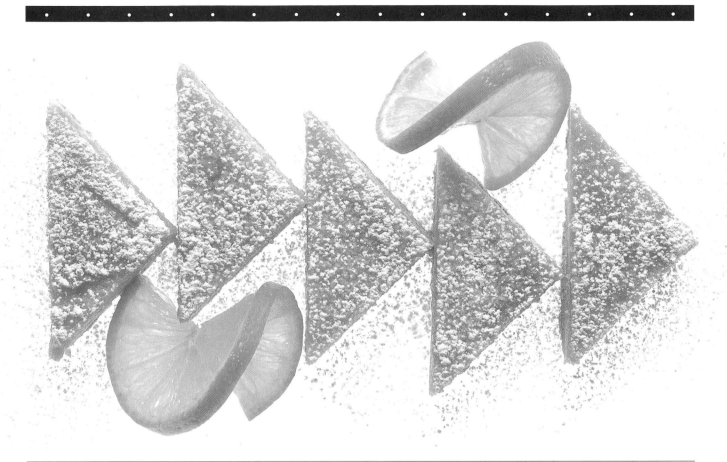

CRUST
1 stick (½ cup) salted butter, softened
¼ cup powdered sugar
1 teaspoon vanilla extract
1 cup all-purpose flour

CREAM CHEESE FILLING
8 ounces cream cheese, softened
1½ cups powdered sugar
1 large egg
1 teaspoon lemon extract

LEMON CURD
4 large egg yolks
1 tablespoon cornstarch
¾ cup granulated sugar
¾ cup water
2 medium lemons grated for 2 teaspoons
   lemon peel, and squeezed for ¼ cup fresh
   lemon juice
2 tablespoons salted butter, softened

TOPPING
2 tablespoons powdered sugar

Yield: 12 bars

• Preheat oven to 325°F.

• Prepare the shortbread crust: Cream butter and sugar in a medium bowl with electric mixer set on high speed. Add vanilla and mix until combined. Add flour and mix at low speed until fully incorporated. Press dough evenly into bottom of an 8-by-8-inch baking pan. Refrigerate until firm,

approximately 30 minutes. Prick shortbread crust with fork and bake for 30 minutes or until crust turns golden brown. Cool on rack to room temperature.

• Prepare the cream cheese filling while the crust is baking: Beat cream cheese and sugar until smooth in a medium bowl with electric mixer set on high speed. Add egg and lemon extract and beat on medium speed until light and smooth. Cover bowl tightly and refrigerate.

- Prepare the lemon curd: Blend the egg yolks with the cornstarch and sugar in a medium nonaluminum saucepan. Place over low heat and slowly whisk in water and lemon juice. Increase heat to medium-low and cook, stirring constantly, until mixture thickens enough to coat the back of a spoon. Remove from heat. Add lemon peel and butter and cool for 10 minutes.

- Assemble the bars: Spread chilled cream cheese filling evenly over cooled shortbread crust with spatula. Spread lemon curd evenly over cream cheese filling. Place pan in center of oven. Bake for 30 to 40 minutes or until edges begin to turn light golden brown. Cool to room temperature on rack. Chill in refrigerator for 1 hour before cutting into bars. Dust top with powdered sugar.

Check the lemon curd to see if it has reached the desired consistency. If it thickly coats the back of a spoon, it is ready. Add the butter and lemon peel and proceed as directed.

Granola Date Bars

FILLING

8 ounces chopped dates (about 1½ cups)
½ cup shredded sweetened coconut
¾ cup half-and-half or light cream
1 teaspoon vanilla extract

GRANOLA BASE

2 cups quick oats (not instant)
¾ cup all-purpose flour
1 cup (packed) dark brown sugar
½ teaspoon baking soda
½ teaspoon ground cinnamon
1 stick (½ cup) salted butter, melted

Yield: 16 bars

- Prepare the filling: Heat dates, coconut, and half-and-half in a medium saucepan over medium heat. Stir occasionally until mixture boils and thickens, about 15 minutes. Remove from heat and stir in vanilla. Set aside to cool.

- Prepare the granola base: Combine oats, flour, sugar, soda, and cinnamon in a medium bowl. Mix well with wire whisk. Pour melted butter over dry ingredients and stir with large wooden spoon until thoroughly moistened.

- Press about 3 cups of the granola mixture into bottom of an 8-by-8-inch baking pan. Place in refrigerator for about 30 minutes to harden.

- Preheat oven to 350°F.

- Spread the cooled date filling evenly over the granola base. Sprinkle the remaining granola mixture (about ¾ cup) over the date filling. Bake for 25 to 30 minutes or until the granola topping is slightly browned and crisp. Cool to room temperature before cutting into 2-inch squares.

After the dates, coconut, and half-and-half have come to a boil, continue to cook the mixture until it has thickened. Stir occasionally to prevent sticking.

Coconut Mud Bars

BOTTOM LAYER
1⅓ cups all-purpose flour
½ teaspoon baking powder
Pinch of salt
½ cup (packed) dark brown sugar
1 stick (½ cup) unsalted butter, slightly
  softened and cut into small pieces

GANACHE
10 ounces semisweet chocolate, finely chopped
¾ cup heavy cream

TOPPING
4 tablespoons (¼ cup) unsalted butter,
  softened
½ cup granulated sugar
2 teaspoons vanilla extract
¼ teaspoon coconut extract (optional)
2 large eggs
1½ cups shredded coconut
1½ cups chopped pecans

Yield: 24 bars

• Preheat the oven to 350°F. Lightly grease a 9-by-13-inch baking pan.

• Make the bottom layer: In a medium bowl, combine the flour, baking powder, salt, and brown sugar. With a pastry blender, cut the butter into the dry ingredients until the mixture resembles coarse meal. Press the mixture into the bottom of the prepared pan. Bake for 10 minutes, or until the crust is just set. Place the pan on a rack to cool, but leave the oven on.

• Meanwhile, make the ganache: Place the chocolate in a medium bowl. In a small saucepan, bring the cream to a simmer. Pour the hot cream over the chocolate; let stand for 5 minutes, then stir until smooth. Pour the ganache over the crust and refrigerate for about 15 minutes to set the ganache.

• Prepare the topping: In a medium bowl, cream the butter. Add the granulated sugar, vanilla, and coconut extract, if desired, and beat until blended. Beat in the eggs. Stir in the coconut and pecans.

• Drop the coconut-pecan topping evenly over the ganache and spread gently. Bake for 25 to 30 minutes, or until the top is golden brown. Set the pan on a wire rack to cool. Cut into bars.

Melt the chocolate for the ganache by pouring hot cream over the finely chopped chocolate. Let stand for about 5 minutes, then stir until melted and smooth.

Creamy Peanut Butter Chocolate Bars

CRUST
8 medium-size butter or chocolate
  chip cookies
1 stick (½ cup) salted butter, melted

CHOCOLATE LAYERS
15 ounces milk chocolate chips
  (about 2½ cups)

PEANUT BUTTER FILLING
1½ cups creamy peanut butter
1 stick (½ cup) salted butter, softened
3 cups powdered sugar
2 teaspoons vanilla extract

Yield: 24 to 36 bars

- Preheat oven to 325°F.

- In food processor or blender, process cookies until finely ground. Add butter and mix together completely. Press crumb mixture into bottom of an 8-by-8-inch baking pan and bake for 10 minutes. Cool to room temperature.

- Melt chocolate in double boiler over slightly simmering water. Or microwave the chocolate, stirring every 30 seconds, until completely melted. Pour half of the melted chocolate into the pan and smooth evenly over crust. Place pan in refrigerator. Keep remaining chocolate warm.

- Prepare the peanut butter filling: Blend peanut butter and butter together until smooth using a food processor or an electric mixer. Slowly beat in powdered sugar and then add vanilla. Beat until smooth. Spread peanut butter filling over the chilled chocolate layer. Finish by pouring remaining warm chocolate over filling and spreading smooth. Chill in refrigerator for 1 hour or until firm. Cut into bars to serve.

Spoon the peanut butter filling over the chilled chocolate and cookie base (far left), then spread smooth. Complete the bar by pouring the melted chocolate over the peanut butter layer (left), spreading it smooth, and chilling in the refrigerator until firm.

112

Vermont Maple Walnut Bars

BARS

2 cups all-purpose flour
½ teaspoon baking soda
½ cup (packed) light brown sugar
1 stick (½ cup) salted butter, softened
1 cup pure maple syrup
1 large egg
2 teaspoons vanilla extract
4 ounces walnuts, chopped (about 1 cup)

MAPLE FROSTING

1 stick (½ cup) salted butter, softened
2 ounces cream cheese, softened
1 tablespoon (packed) light brown sugar
3 tablespoons pure maple syrup
¼ cup plus 2 tablespoons powdered sugar
Walnut halves (optional)

Yield: 12 to 16 bars

- Preheat oven to 325°F. Grease an 8-by-8-inch baking pan.

- Make bars: In a medium bowl, combine flour and soda. Mix well with a wire whisk and set aside.

- In a large bowl with an electric mixer, blend sugar and butter to form a grainy paste. Scrape down sides of bowl, then add syrup, egg and vanilla. Beat at medium speed until smooth.

- Add the flour mixture and walnuts, and blend at low speed just until combined. Do not overmix.

- Pour batter into baking pan and smooth top with a spatula. Bake for 40 to 45 minutes or until toothpick inserted into center comes out clean. Cool in pan 15 minutes, then invert onto cooling rack. Cool completely before icing.

- Make frosting: In a medium bowl, cream butter and cream cheese with electric mixer at high speed. Add brown sugar and maple syrup, and beat until smooth. Reduce mixer speed to medium, and slowly add powdered sugar. Once sugar is incorporated, increase speed to high, and mix until smooth. If frosting appears thin, gradually add powdered sugar until frosting thickens.

- Using a metal spatula, spread frosting on top and sides of maple bars. If desired, make designs on frosting or decorate with walnut halves.

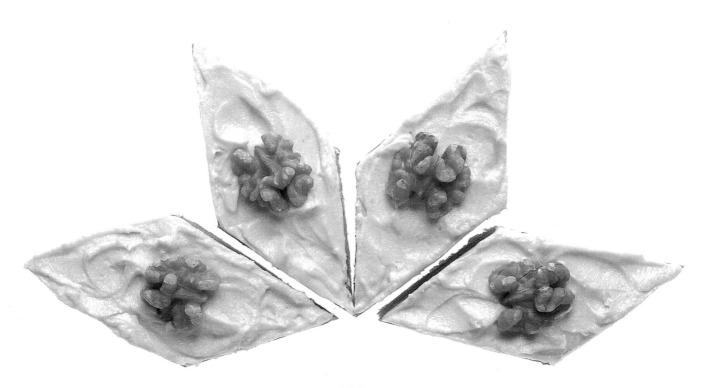

Tuxedo Cookie Bars

1½ cups all-purpose flour
1 teaspoon baking soda
1 stick (½ cup) salted butter
1½ cups granulated sugar
18 ounces semisweet chocolate chips
  (about 3 cups)
1 tablespoon vanilla extract

4 tablespoons hot water
4 large eggs
6 ounces white chocolate chips
  (about 1 cup)

Yield: 18 bars

- Preheat oven to 325°F. Grease a 9-by-13-inch baking pan.

- In a medium bowl, combine flour and soda with a wire whisk, and set aside.

- In a small saucepan, melt butter and 2 cups of the semisweet chips over low heat, stirring constantly until smooth.

- In a large bowl with an electric mixer at medium speed, beat chocolate mixture and sugar until smooth, about 5 minutes. Continuing to beat, add the vanilla, then the water, a tablespoon at a time.

Scrape down sides of bowl. Next, add eggs one at a time, mixing well after each addition.

- Gradually add the flour mixture, blending at low speed. Then add the remaining 1 cup of semisweet chips and the white chocolate chips. Blend until equally distributed throughout the batter.

- Spread batter into prepared baking pan. Bake for 35 to 40 minutes or until toothpick inserted into center comes out just slightly moist.

- Cool to room temperature. Cover well and refrigerate until cold. Cut into bars to serve.

Mother Lode Brownies

BROWNIE LAYER
¾ cup all-purpose flour
¼ teaspoon baking soda
3 ounces unsweetened chocolate
3 ounces semisweet chocolate
1½ sticks (¾ cup) unsalted butter
1½ cups (packed) light brown sugar
3 large eggs
2 teaspoons vanilla extract

CARAMEL LAYER
¾ cup granulated sugar
3 tablespoons water
¼ cup heavy cream, scalded
2 tablespoons unsalted butter

TOPPINGS
1 cup coarsely chopped macadamia nuts
9 ounces semisweet chocolate chips
   (about 1½ cups)
6 ounces milk chocolate chips
   (about 1 cup)

Yield: 16 brownies

- Preheat the oven to 325°F. Grease and flour a 9-by-9-inch baking pan.

- Make the brownie layer: In a small bowl, combine the flour and baking soda.

- In a double boiler, melt the unsweetened chocolate and the semisweet chocolate with the butter. Stir until smooth and set aside to cool slightly. In a large bowl with an electric mixer, beat the brown sugar and eggs until lightened and pale in color. Beat in the cooled chocolate mixture and the vanilla. Gradually beat in the flour mixture. Pour the batter into the prepared pan. Bake for 40 to 50 minutes, or until the center is set but still moist and a bit fudgy. Cool in the pan on a wire rack.

- Prepare the caramel layer: In a small, heavy saucepan, dissolve the sugar in the water over low heat, stirring constantly. Bring to a boil over medium-high heat, then let boil without stirring until the syrup turns a deep amber. While the syrup is boiling, brush down the sides of the pan from time to time with a wet pastry brush to prevent crystals from forming. Remove the pan from the heat, then stir in the hot cream (be careful, it will bubble rapidly). Continue stirring, over low heat if necessary, until all of the caramel is dissolved into the cream. Stir in the butter until smooth. Set the caramel aside until it has cooled slightly but is still spreadable.

- Assemble: Preheat the oven to 325°F. Spread the caramel over the cooled brownies. Sprinkle the toppings over the caramel layer and place the brownies in the oven for 5 minutes to set the toppings (do not let the chips melt completely).

- Set on a wire rack to cool, then cut into squares.

Chocolate Chip Biscotti

3 cups all-purpose flour
½ cup unsweetened cocoa powder
¾ teaspoon baking powder
⅛ teaspoon salt
3 tablespoons unsalted butter
¾ cup granulated sugar

3 large eggs
1 tablespoon grated orange zest
1 teaspoon vanilla extract
1 cup mini semisweet chocolate chips

Yield: About 3 dozen

- Preheat the oven to 350°F. Spray a baking sheet with nonstick cooking spray.

- In a medium bowl, combine the flour, cocoa, baking powder, and salt and set aside. In another medium bowl with an electric mixer, cream the butter and sugar. Beat in the eggs, one at a time. Beat in the vanilla. Gradually mix in the dry ingredients and orange zest, beating until fully incorporated. Stir in the chocolate chips.

- Divide the dough in half and shape each piece into a log 9 inches long and 3 inches wide. Place the logs on the prepared baking sheet and bake for 30 minutes, or until set. Transfer the logs to a rack and let cool slightly, about 10 minutes. Turn the oven down to 200°F.

- Place the still-warm logs on a cutting board and, with a serrated knife, cut each log on the diagonal into ½-inch slices. Lay the slices on a baking sheet and bake for 5 minutes. Carefully turn the biscotti and bake for another 10 minutes, or until crisp. Transfer to a rack to cool.

After the baked biscotti logs have cooled slightly, cut them with a serrated knife into ½-inch slices. Lay the slices on a baking sheet and bake until crisp.

Caramel-Filled Brownies

BROWNIES
3 ounces unsweetened chocolate
1 stick (½ cup) salted butter, softened
4 large eggs
1½ cups granulated sugar
1 tablespoon vanilla extract
1½ cups all-purpose flour

CARAMEL
½ stick (¼ cup) salted butter
⅓ cup (packed) dark brown sugar
2 tablespoons light corn syrup
1 tablespoon whipping cream

Yield: 16 brownies

- Preheat oven to 325°F. Grease an 8-by-8-inch baking pan.

- In a small saucepan, melt chocolate and ½ cup butter over low heat, stirring constantly. Remove from heat.

- Beat eggs in a large bowl using an electric mixer set on high speed until they thicken slightly. Add sugar slowly. Add vanilla and mix well. Add chocolate-butter mixture, and beat on medium until uniformly brown. Add the flour and blend at low speed until just combined. Do not overmix.

- Pour half of the brownie batter into the prepared pan. Smooth top. Bake for 15 to 20 minutes or until top is firm.

- Prepare the carmel: Heat butter, sugar, and corn syrup in heavy pan over medium heat, stirring constantly until sugar dissolves. Increase heat to high and boil 1½ minutes. Remove from heat and stir in cream. Keep warm.

- Spread warm caramel evenly over top of baked brownie layer. Pour remaining half of brownie mixture over caramel, smoothing the top. Bake an additional 25 to 30 minutes or until toothpick inserted into center comes cleanly out of top brownie layer. (Some caramel may stick to the toothpick.)

- Cool brownies in pan, then cut into squares. Serve at room temperature or chilled.

117

Brownie Nuggets

BROWNIES
6 ounces semisweet chocolate chips
  (about 1 cup)
1 stick (½ cup) unsalted butter
½ cup plus 2 tablespoons all-purpose flour
¼ teaspoon salt
2 large eggs
¾ cup (packed) light brown sugar
1 teaspoon vanilla extract

WHITE CHOCOLATE GANACHE
9 ounces white chocolate, finely chopped
½ cup heavy cream
1 tablespoon unsalted butter

Yield: About 2 dozen

- Preheat the oven to 350°F. Line 24 mini-muffin cups with paper liners.

- Make the brownies: In a double boiler, melt the chocolate chips with the butter, stirring until smooth. Set aside to cool to room temperature.

- In a small bowl, whisk together the flour and salt.

- In a medium bowl, beat the eggs and sugar until thick and pale. Stir in the vanilla and the cooled chocolate mixture until well blended. Stir in the flour mixture until just combined.

- Dividing evenly, spoon the batter into the muffin cups. Bake for 12 to 15 minutes, or until the edges are set but the centers are still moist and fudgy.

- Cool the brownies in the pan on a rack for 15 minutes. Remove from the pan to cool completely.

- Prepare the ganache: Place the white chocolate in a medium bowl. In a small saucepan, bring the cream to a simmer. Pour the hot cream over the chocolate. Let stand, covered, for 5 minutes, then stir until smooth. Stir in the butter until incorporated and smooth. Refrigerate the ganache until it is thickened but still pourable.

- Dip the brownie nuggets: Dip the tops of the brownies in the ganache. Refrigerate to set the ganache. Dip the brownies in the ganache again for a second coat. Chill to set the ganache.

Reduced-Fat Chocolate Brownies

½ cup water
3 ounces pitted prunes
  (about 9 prunes)
¾ cup plus 1 tablespoon all-purpose flour
½ cup unsweetened cocoa powder
½ teaspoon baking powder
¼ teaspoon salt
½ stick (¼ cup) unsalted butter

1 cup (packed) light brown sugar
½ cup unsweetened applesauce
2 teaspoons vanilla extract
4 egg whites
¼ cup mini semisweet chocolate chips
  (optional)

Yield: 16 brownies

- Preheat the oven to 325°F. Spray an 8-by-8-inch baking pan with nonstick cooking spray.

- In a small, heavy saucepan, bring the water to a boil. Add the prunes, cover, reduce the heat, and simmer for 5 minutes. Remove from the heat and set aside to steep for 5 minutes. Uncover and let cool to room temperature. Drain the liquid and purée the prunes.

- In a small bowl, whisk together the flour, cocoa, baking powder, and salt.

- In a medium bowl with an electric mixer, cream the butter and sugar. Beat in the prune purée, applesauce, and vanilla. Beat in the egg whites. Beat in the flour mixture.

- Spread the batter in the prepared pan and smooth the top. Sprinkle with the chocolate chips, if desired. Bake for 35 to 40 minutes, or until the center springs back when lightly pressed; do not overbake.

- Cool in the pan on a rack, then cut into 16 squares.

Super Fudge Brownies

6 ounces unsweetened baking chocolate
2 sticks (1 cup) salted butter, softened
4 large eggs
2 cups granulated sugar
1 tablespoon vanilla extract
½ cup all-purpose flour

6 ounces semisweet chocolate chips
(about 1 cup)

Yield: 16 brownies, 2 inches square

- Preheat oven to 300°F. Grease an 8-by-8-inch baking pan.

- Combine unsweetened baking chocolate and butter in a medium saucepan. Melt over medium-low heat, stirring constantly until pieces are almost melted. Remove from heat and stir until smooth.

- In a large bowl, using an electric mixer on medium speed, beat eggs until light yellow in color—about 5 minutes. Add sugar and blend on low until thoroughly combined.

- Add vanilla and melted chocolate to the egg and sugar mixture. Blend on low speed until smooth. Add the flour and mix thoroughly.

- Pour batter into greased pan. Smooth surface with a spatula, and sprinkle uniformly with chocolate chips. Bake on the center rack of oven for 45 to 55 minutes. The batter should be set and a toothpick inserted into the center should come out clean. Do not overbake.

- Cool to room temperature. Cover and refrigerate for at least 1 hour. Cut and serve chilled.

Twice-Topped Brownies

BROWNIE LAYER
4 ounces unsweetened chocolate
1 stick (½ cup) salted butter
¾ cup all-purpose flour
¼ teaspoon salt
2 large eggs
1 cup (packed) light brown sugar
2 teaspoons vanilla extract
½ cup chopped pecans
½ cup mini semisweet chocolate chips

VANILLA CREAM
1 stick (½ cup) salted butter, softened
4 ounces cream cheese, softened
1 teaspoon vanilla extract
1¼ cups powdered sugar

CHOCOLATE DRIZZLE
2 ounces semisweet chocolate chips
2 tablespoons heavy cream

Yield: 16 brownies

- Preheat the oven to 325°F. Grease a 7-by-11-inch baking pan.

- Prepare the brownie layer: In a double boiler, melt the unsweetened chocolate and butter together, stirring until smooth. Set aside to cool slightly.

- In a small bowl, combine the flour and salt.

- In a medium bowl, beat the eggs and brown sugar together. Beat in the chocolate mixture and the vanilla. Stir in the flour mixture. Then stir in the pecans and mini chocolate chips.

- Spread the batter in the prepared pan and bake for 22 to 25 minutes, or until a cake tester inserted into the center comes out clean. Cool in the pan on a rack.

- Make the vanilla cream: In a medium bowl, cream the butter and cream cheese until light and fluffy. Gradually beat in the vanilla and powdered sugar. Spread the vanilla cream over the cooled brownies. Refrigerate until set.

- Prepare the drizzle: In a double boiler, melt the chocolate chips and cream over hot, not simmering, water. Stir until smooth, then set aside to cool slightly. Dip a fork into the melted chocolate mixture and drizzle in a random pattern over the vanilla cream layer.

- Chill until ready to serve.

Brownies Espresso

BROWNIES
2½ cups all-purpose flour
½ teaspoon baking soda
1 cup (packed) dark brown sugar
½ cup granulated sugar
2 sticks (1 cup) salted butter, softened
2 ounces unsweetened baking chocolate
1 tablespoon instant espresso or instant
  coffee granules
1 tablespoon boiling water
2 large eggs

1 teaspoon vanilla extract
1 teaspoon almond extract
1 cup (6 ounces) semisweet chocolate chips

GLAZE
3 ounces semisweet chocolate
⅓ cup salted butter, softened
½ cup sliced almonds

Yield: 12 to 16 servings

- Preheat oven to 325°F. Grease an 8-by-8-inch baking pan.

- In a medium bowl combine flour and soda. Mix well with a wire whisk and set aside.

- In a large bowl blend sugars with an electric mixer at medium speed. Add butter and mix to form a grainy paste.

- Melt baking chocolate in a double boiler. Meanwhile, in a small bowl, dissolve espresso or coffee granules in boiling water.

- Add chocolate and coffee to sugar and butter; beat at medium speed until smooth. Add eggs, vanilla and almond extracts; beat until smooth.

- Scrape down sides of bowl. Add the flour mixture and chocolate chips, and blend at low speed just until combined. Do not overmix.

- Pour batter into greased baking pan. Bake for 35 to 40 minutes or until toothpick placed in center comes out clean. Cool in pan for 15 minutes. Invert on rack.

- To make glaze: Melt together the chocolate and butter in a double boiler, stirring until smooth.

- Spread glaze over brownies and sprinkle with almonds. Cool completely before cutting into bars.

Pies, Cakes, and Pastries

Mousse-Filled Cookie Pie

CRUST

1¼ cups all-purpose flour
¼ cup unsweetened cocoa powder
½ teaspoon baking soda
1 stick (½ cup) unsalted butter
½ cup (packed) light brown sugar
¼ cup granulated sugar
1 large egg, at room temperature
1 cup mini semisweet chocolate chips

MOUSSE FILLING

2 cups heavy cream
2 teaspoons unflavored gelatin
8 ounces white chocolate, coarsely chopped
1 teaspoon almond extract
Large white and dark Chocolate Scrolls
  (page 229), for garnish

Yield: One 9-inch pie

- Preheat the oven to 350°F. Lightly butter a 9-inch pie plate.

- Make the crust: In a small bowl, whisk together the flour, cocoa powder, and baking soda.

- In a medium bowl with an electric mixer, cream the butter with the brown and granulated sugars. Beat in the egg. On low speed, gradually beat in the flour mixture until just combined. Stir in the chocolate chips.

- Press the dough evenly into the prepared pie plate and chill in the refrigerator for 15 minutes. Bake for 15 to 20 minutes, or just until set. Set aside to cool to room temperature.

- Meanwhile, make the mousse filling: Place ¼ cup of the cream in a small bowl. Sprinkle the gelatin on top and let stand for 5 minutes to soften.

- Place the white chocolate in a medium bowl. In a medium saucepan, bring 1 cup of the cream to a simmer. Pour the hot cream over the chocolate. Let stand, covered, for 5 minutes, then stir until smooth. Whisk in the softened gelatin and almond extract. Set aside to cool to lukewarm.

- In a medium bowl, beat the remaining ¾ cup cream until soft peaks form. Gently whisk about ½ cup of the whipped cream into the chocolate mixture to lighten it. Gently but thoroughly fold in the remaining whipped cream. Spoon the mousse filling into the crust. Refrigerate the pie for at least 3 hours to set.

- Serve garnished with large white and dark Chocolate Scrolls.

Chocolate Angel Pie

MERINGUE SHELL
4 large egg whites
¼ teaspoon salt
¼ teaspoon cream of tartar
1 cup granulated sugar
⅓ cup hazelnuts—toasted, skinned and
  finely chopped

FILLING
¼ cup granulated sugar
3 tablespoons cornstarch
½ teaspoon salt
1½ cups milk
6 ounces semisweet chocolate, finely chopped
1¼ cups heavy cream
Chocolate shavings, whole hazelnuts, and
  powdered sugar, for garnish

Yield: One 9-inch pie

- Preheat the oven to 275F°.

- Make the meringue shell: In a medium bowl, beat the egg whites, salt, and cream of tartar until foamy. Gradually add the sugar and beat until stiff, glossy peaks form. Spread the meringue over the bottom and up the sides of a 9-inch pie plate. Build the meringue up around the rim, extending it 1 inch higher than the rim.

- Sprinkle the chopped hazelnuts over the bottom of the crust. Bake for 35 minutes, or until the meringue is dry and light golden. Let the meringue shell stand in the oven with the heat turned off and the door ajar for 1 hour.

- Meanwhile, make the filling: In a medium saucepan, combine the sugar, cornstarch, and salt. Stir in the milk until well blended. Bring the mixture to a boil over medium heat, stirring constantly. Boil, stirring, for 1 minute. Remove the pan from the heat. Add the chocolate and stir until melted and smooth. Transfer the mixture to a bowl; cool to room temperature.

- In a medium bowl, beat the cream until stiff peaks form. Gently and thoroughly fold the cream into the chocolate mixture. Spoon the filling into the meringue shell. Refrigerate the pie for about 30 minutes before serving.

- Garnish the pie with chocolate shavings and whole hazelnuts dusted with powdered sugar.

Baby Banana Cream Pies

PASTRY
1½ cups all-purpose flour
2 tablespoons granulated sugar
1 stick (½ cup) salted butter, chilled and cut
  into 8 pieces
1 teaspoon vanilla extract
4 to 5 tablespoons ice water

PASTRY CREAM
2 cups light cream
One 1-inch piece vanilla bean, split in
  half lengthwise or 2 teaspoons
  vanilla extract
½ cup granulated sugar

2 tablespoons all-purpose flour
4 large egg yolks, lightly beaten
2 tablespoons salted butter
1 teaspoon crème de bananes liqueur or
  1 teaspoon pure banana extract

TOPPING
1 cup heavy cream
¼ cup powdered sugar
½ teaspoon vanilla extract
2 large or 3 medium bananas, cut into
  thin slices

Yield: 12 baby banana pies

- To prepare pastry: In medium bowl combine flour, sugar and butter with a pastry cutter until dough resembles coarse meal. Add water and vanilla with fork and mix until dough can be shaped into a ball. Or use a food processor fitted with metal blade to combine flour, sugar and butter until dough resembles coarse meal. Add vanilla and sugar and butter until dough resembles coarse meal. Add vanilla and water gradually and process just until a ball forms. Tightly wrap dough in plastic wrap or plastic bag and place in refrigerator 1 hour or until firm.

- To prepare the pastry cream: Scald cream with vanilla bean in heavy saucepan set over medium heat. Remove from heat. In small bowl whisk together the sugar and flour. Slowly pour the sugar-

flour mixture into the hot cream, whisking constantly. Place saucepan back over medium heat, stirring constantly until mixture thickens enough to coat the back of a spoon.

- Temper egg yolks by pouring 1 cup of hot cream mixture into yolks, stirring briskly. Pour warmed egg mixture into saucepan and continue cooking over medium heat. Stir constantly until mixture thickens enough to coat the back of a spoon. Do not boil.

- Remove from heat and transfer filling to bowl. If using vanilla extract, stir it in along with the butter and banana liqueur. Cover with plastic wrap and chill thoroughly in refrigerator.

- Preheat oven to 400°F.

- On floured board using a floured rolling pin, roll out dough to ⅛-inch thickness. Cut out 4-inch rounds and press into bottoms and up sides of muffin tin. Reuse dough scraps until all cups have been lined. Chill dough in refrigerator 15 minutes.

- Prick dough on bottom and sides with fork. Bake for 15 minutes or until pastry begins to turn golden brown. Remove from oven and cool to room temperature.

- To prepare the whipped cream: Beat cream with powdered sugar and vanilla with an electric mixer set on high speed until stiff peaks form.

- Assemble the pies by placing 2 thin banana slices in bottom of each pastry shell. Top with pastry cream, add more banana slices and top with whipped cream. Serve immediately.

Cut 4-inch rounds out of the pastry dough (above). Press the rounds into the cups of a medium- to large-size muffin tin (right). Repeat the procedure until you have lined 12 cups. Prick the sides and bottom of the dough with a fork, then bake as directed.

Caramel Fudge Mac Tart

PASTRY
½ cup macadamia nuts
¼ cup granulated sugar
¾ cup all-purpose flour
4 tablespoons cold unsalted butter
1 egg yolk
1 tablespoon water
1 teaspoon vanilla extract

CARAMEL LAYER
¾ cup granulated sugar
¼ cup water
½ cup heavy cream, scalded

2 tablespoons unsalted butter, at room
  temperature

CHOCOLATE FUDGE LAYER
½ cup heavy cream
1 egg yolk
1 tablespoon granulated sugar
3 tablespoons sour cream
6 ounces semisweet chocolate, finely chopped
1 teaspoon vanilla extract
Chopped toasted macadamia nuts, for garnish

Yield: One 9-inch tart

- Make the pastry: In a food processor, grind the macadamia nuts with the sugar into small pieces. Add the flour and butter, then process until the dough resembles coarse meal. In a small bowl, lightly beat the egg yolk with the water and vanilla. With the machine running, add the egg yolk mixture and process until the dough gathers into a ball.

- Lightly butter a 9-inch tart pan with a removable bottom. Scrape the dough into the pan and press into the bottom and up the sides. Cover and refrigerate for 30 minutes.

- Meanwhile, make the caramel layer: In a small heavy saucepan, dissolve the sugar in the water over low heat, stirring constantly. Bring to a boil over medium-high heat, then let boil without stirring until the syrup turns a light amber. While the syrup is boiling, brush down the sides of the pan from time to time with a wet pastry brush to prevent crystals from forming. Remove the pan from the heat and stir in the hot cream (be careful, it will bubble rapidly). Continue stirring, over low heat if

necessary, until all of the caramel is dissolved into the cream. Stir in the butter and set aside to cool to room temperature.

- Preheat the oven to 350°F. Prick the tart dough all over with a fork and bake for 18 minutes, or until the crust is golden. Cool to room temperature.

- Meanwhile, make the chocolate fudge layer: In a heavy medium saucepan, stir together the cream, egg yolk, sugar, and sour cream over medium heat. Stir lightly until the mixture just begins to scald. Remove from the heat, stir in the chocolate and vanilla, and blend until smooth. Pour the fudge into the cooled crust.

- Pour three-fourths of the cooled caramel over the fudge layer. Top the caramel layer with chopped macadamia nuts. Drizzle the remaining caramel over the nuts.

- Cover the tart and chill in the refrigerator to set. Let the tart sit at room temperature for 20 minutes before serving.

Chocolate Mousse Tart

CRUST

1 large egg yolk
2 tablespoons ice water
1 teaspoon vanilla extract
1¼ cups all-purpose flour
¼ cup granulated sugar
6 tablespoons cold unsalted butter, cut
 into pieces

FILLING

3 ounces coarsely chopped semisweet
 chocolate plus 9 ounces finely chopped
 semisweet chocolate
2 cups heavy cream
¼ cup powdered sugar
1 teaspoon vanilla extract
Whipped cream and Chocolate Scrolls
 (page 229), for garnish

Yield: 8 servings

- Make the crust: In a small bowl, combine the egg yolk, water, and vanilla. In a medium bowl, whisk together the flour and sugar.

- Cut the butter into the flour-sugar mixture until it resembles coarse meal. Stir in the egg yolk mixture. If the dough does not mass together, add up to 1 more tablespoon water, a bit at a time. Shape the dough into a disk, wrap in plastic, and chill for 1 hour.

- Preheat the oven to 400°F. Remove the dough from the refrigerator and let stand for 10 minutes, then roll it into an 11-inch round. Fit it into a 9-inch tart pan with a removable bottom. Freeze for 15 minutes.

- Prick the tart shell in several places with a fork. Line the shell with aluminum foil and fill with dried beans, rice, or metal pie weights and then bake for 5 minutes. Remove the foil and weights, and bake for 15 minutes longer, or until golden brown. Set the tart shell on a wire rack to cool to room temperature.

- Make the filling: In a double boiler, melt the 3 ounces of coarsely chopped chocolate over hot, not simmering, water. Pour the melted chocolate into the bottom of the cooled crust; chill while you make the mousse.

- In a small saucepan, bring ½ cup of the cream to a simmer. Remove the pan from the heat and stir in 6 ounces of the finely chopped chocolate. Cover and set aside for 5 minutes, then stir the mixture until smooth. Transfer the chocolate cream to a large bowl.

- In another large bowl, whip the remaining 1½ cups cream with the powdered sugar and vanilla until soft peaks form. Fold one-third of the cream into the chocolate mixture to lighten it. Stir in the remaining 3 ounces chopped chocolate, then gently fold in the remaining whipped cream.

- To assemble: Spread the mousse evenly in the tart shell. Chill until serving time. Garnish with whipped cream and Chocolate Scrolls.

Double-Chocolate Silk Pie

CRUST
1½ cups chocolate wafer crumbs
6 tablespoons unsalted butter, melted

FILLING
1½ cups heavy cream
3 tablespoons granulated sugar
Pinch of salt

5 large egg yolks
10 ounces semisweet chocolate, finely
  chopped
1½ teaspoons vanilla extract
Chocolate Scrolls (page 229) and whipped
  cream, for garnish

Yield: One 9-inch pie

- Make the crust: In a medium bowl, combine the crumbs and melted butter. Press the crumb mixture into the bottom and up the sides of a 9-inch pie plate. Chill while you make the filling.

- Prepare the filling: In a double boiler, scald the cream; stir in the sugar and salt. In a small bowl, lightly beat the yolks. Whisk about ¼ cup of the hot cream into the yolks to warm them. Transfer the warmed eggs to the double boiler and cook over simmering water, whisking constantly, until the custard just begins to thicken and coats the back of a spoon, 8 to 9 minutes. Remove from the heat and add the chocolate and vanilla. Stir until the chocolate melts and the custard is smooth.

- Pour the custard filling into the pie crust. Cool to room temperature. Place a piece of plastic wrap directly on the filling to prevent a skin from forming. Refrigerate the pie overnight to set the filling. Remove the plastic wrap and smooth the top of the pie. Garnish with Chocolate Scrolls and rosettes of whipped cream.

To prevent a skin from forming on the pie filling, place a sheet of plastic wrap directly on its surface.

Chocolate Banana Cream Pie

CRUST
1 cup all-purpose flour
2 tablespoons granulated sugar
½ teaspoon salt
6 tablespoons cold unsalted butter, cut
  into pieces
1 egg yolk
2 tablespoons ice water

FILLING
¾ cup granulated sugar
5 tablespoons cornstarch
¼ teaspoon salt

1½ cups heavy cream
1 cup milk
5 large egg yolks
2 large eggs
6 ounces semisweet chocolate,
  coarsely chopped
2 teaspoons vanilla extract
3 medium bananas
1 tablespoon fresh lemon juice
Whipped cream, for garnish

Yield: 8 to 10 servings

- Prepare the crust: In a food processor, combine the flour, sugar, and salt and process briefly to combine. Add the butter and process until the mixture resembles coarse meal. With the machine running, add the egg yolk and ice water and process just until the dough masses together. Gather the dough into a ball, flatten into a large disk, and then press into a 9-inch pie plate; trim and crimp the edges. Freeze for 10 minutes.

- Preheat the oven to 425°F. Line the pie crust loosely with foil and fill with dried beans, rice or metal pie weights. Bake for 10 minutes. Reduce the oven temperature to 350°F, remove the weights and bake for 10 minutes longer, or until golden brown. Set the crust on a wire rack to cool completely.

- Make the filling: In a saucepan, combine the sugar, cornstarch, salt, cream, and milk. Bring to a simmer over medium heat, stirring constantly to dissolve the sugar, about 12 minutes. Remove from the heat.

- In a small bowl, beat the egg yolks and eggs. Whisk about ¼ cup of the cream mixture into the eggs to warm them. Transfer the warmed eggs to the saucepan. Cook over medium heat, stirring constantly, until the custard is of pudding consistency, about 6 minutes; do not boil. Remove from the heat, add the chocolate, and let stand for 1 minute. Add vanilla and stir until the chocolate is melted.

- Spread half of the custard in the cooled pie crust. Slice and arrange 1½ bananas over the custard. Top with the remaining custard. Slice the remaining 1½ bananas and toss the slices with the lemon juice; drain well. Arrange the banana slices over the custard. Cover the pie with plastic wrap and refrigerate until well chilled, about 4 hours.

- Serve the pie garnished with rosettes of whipped cream.

Classic Apple Pie

CRUST
3 cups all-purpose flour
2 teaspoons grated lemon zest
  (1 medium lemon)
2 sticks (1 cup) salted butter, chilled
6 to 8 tablespoons ice water

FILLING
6 large Granny Smith apples, peeled and
  thinly sliced (about 4 cups)
1 cup granulated sugar

1 teaspoon ground cinnamon
¼ cup cornstarch
½ stick (¼ cup) salted butter, chilled and cut
  into small pieces

EGG WASH
1 large egg, beaten
1 tablespoon granulated sugar

Yield: 8 slices

- To prepare crust: Mix flour and lemon zest together with wire whisk in a medium bowl. With pastry cutter or 2 knives, cut in butter with flour until dough resembles coarse meal.

- Add ice water and blend until dough can be gathered into a ball. Divide dough in half, flatten into disks, and wrap tightly in plastic wrap or a plastic bag. Refrigerate 1 hour or until firm.

- To prepare filling: Combine sugar, cinnamon and cornstarch with a wire whisk in a large bowl. Add apples to sugar mixture and toss with a wooden spoon until dry ingredients coat the apples

completely.

- Preheat oven to 400°F.

- On a floured surface use a floured rolling pin to roll out one piece of dough into a circle 11 inches in diameter. Fold the crust in half, then in quarters.

- Place point of folded crust in center of a 9-inch pie plate and carefully unfold. Trim excess dough, leaving about ¾ inch hanging over edge of plate

- Spoon in the apple filling and sprinkle the butter pieces on top.

- To prepare top crust: Roll out second piece of

dough into a circle 10 inches in diameter. Again, fold in half, then quarters, and place on top of filling. Fold extra crust of the top layer over the bottom layer. Crimp layers together decoratively.

- Cut several steam slits in pie top, brush with egg wash, and sprinkle with 1 tablespoon sugar.

- Place pie on center rack of oven. Bake for 20 minutes, then reduce heat to 350°F. Bake an additional 30 minutes, or until crust is deep golden brown and filling is bubbling through steam slits.

- Remove from oven and cool to room temperature on rack.

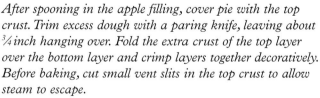

After spooning in the apple filling, cover pie with the top crust. Trim excess dough with a paring knife, leaving about ¾ inch hanging over. Fold the extra crust of the top layer over the bottom layer and crimp layers together decoratively. Before baking, cut small vent slits in the top crust to allow steam to escape.

Chocolate Coconut Pecan Pie

CRUST
1 cup all-purpose flour
⅛ teaspoon salt
6 tablespoons cold unsalted butter, cut
  into pieces
2 to 3 tablespoons ice water

FILLING AND TOPPING
2 tablespoons all-purpose flour
¼ teaspoon baking powder
¼ teaspoon salt
½ stick (¼ cup) unsalted butter

¾ cup (packed) light brown sugar
4 large egg yolks
2 teaspoons vanilla extract
1 cup shredded coconut
1 cup coarsely chopped pecans
4 ounces semisweet chocolate,
  coarsely chopped
¾ cup heavy cream
Whole pecans and whipped cream,
  for garnish

Yield: One 9-inch pie

- Make the crust: In a small bowl, whisk together the flour and salt. With a pastry blender, incorporate the butter into the flour until the mixture resembles coarse meal. Toss the mixture with a fork, sprinkling on just enough of the ice water to form a cohesive dough. Flatten the dough into a disk, wrap in plastic wrap, and chill in the refrigerator for 30 minutes. Roll out to a 12-inch circle and fit into a 9-inch pie plate. Trim and crimp the edges. Return to the refrigerator while you make the filling.

- Preheat the oven to 350°F.

- Prepare the filling: In a small bowl, whisk together the flour, baking powder, and salt. In a medium bowl with an electric mixer, cream the butter and sugar. Beat in the egg yolks and the vanilla. Slowly beat in the flour mixture. Stir in the coconut, pecans, and half of the chopped chocolate. Blend in the cream until smooth.

- Pour the filling into the pie crust and sprinkle with the remaining chopped chocolate. Bake for 40 to 45 minutes, or until the crust is golden brown. The center of the filling will still be a bit jiggly. Let cool to room temperature, then chill for 2 hours to set.

- Garnish each slice of pie with a whole pecan and a whipped cream rosette.

Peanut Butter Cream Pie

CHOCOLATE CRUST
6 ounces semisweet chocolate chips
   (about 1 cup)
5 tablespoons unsalted butter
2½ cups crisp rice cereal
¼ cup mini semisweet chocolate chips

FILLING
8 ounces cream cheese, softened
One 14-ounce can sweetened condensed milk

¾ cup creamy peanut butter
2 teaspoons vanilla extract
1 cup heavy cream

TOPPING
3 ounces milk chocolate, finely chopped
2 tablespoons heavy cream
Milk chocolate curls, for garnish

Yield: One 9-inch pie

- Make the crust: In a double boiler, melt the 6 ounces of chocolate chips and butter over low heat. Remove from the heat and stir until smooth. Gently stir in the rice cereal until completely coated. Set aside to cool to lukewarm, then stir in the mini chips. Press into the bottom and up the sides of a buttered 9-inch pie plate. Chill for 30 minutes to set the chocolate.

- Prepare the filling: In a large bowl with an electric mixer, beat the cream cheese until fluffy. Beat in the condensed milk, peanut butter, and vanilla.

- In a medium bowl, beat the heavy cream until soft peaks form. Fold the whipped cream into the peanut butter mixture. Pour the filling into the crust.

- Make the topping: In a double boiler, melt the milk chocolate over hot, not simmering, water. Add the heavy cream and stir constantly until blended. Set aside to cool slightly, then drizzle the chocolate over the top of the pie. Refrigerate until firm, about 2 hours. Garnish with milk chocolate curls.

Use a spatula to fold whipped cream into the cream cheese-peanut butter mixture.

Chocolate Pumpkin Pie

CRUST
6 tablespoons cold unsalted butter
1 cup all-purpose flour
¼ teaspoon salt
2 to 3 tablespoons ice water

PUMPKIN FILLING
1 cup (packed) light brown sugar
1 tablespoon plus 1 teaspoon
  all-purpose flour
1 teaspoon cinnamon
¼ teaspoon grated nutmeg
¼ teaspoon salt
½ teaspoon ground ginger
⅛ teaspoon ground cloves

1 large egg
1 large egg white
2 tablespoons vanilla extract
One 15-ounce can unsweetened solid-pack
  pumpkin purée
1 cup light cream or half-and-half

CHOCOLATE TOPPING
4 ounces semisweet chocolate,
  coarsely chopped
½ cup heavy cream
2 tablespoons granulated sugar

Yield: One 9-inch pie

● Make the crust: With a pastry blender, incorporate the butter into the flour until the mixture resembles coarse meal. Toss the mixture with a fork, sprinkling on just enough of the ice water to form a cohesive dough. Flatten the dough into a disk, wrap in plastic wrap, and chill in the refrigerator for 45 minutes. Roll out to an 11-inch circle and fit into a 9-inch pie plate. Trim and crimp the edges. Return to the refrigerator while you make the filling.

● Preheat the oven to 350°F.

● Prepare the pumpkin filling: In a medium bowl with an electric mixer, beat the brown sugar, flour, cinnamon, nutmeg, salt, ginger, and cloves until well mixed. Beat in the egg, egg white, and vanilla

until smooth. Beat in the pumpkin, then the light cream. Pour into the chilled pastry shell. Bake for 40 minutes, or until the center is set. Cool on a rack to room temperature.

● Meanwhile, make the chocolate topping: Place the chocolate in a small bowl. In a small saucepan, bring the heavy cream and the granulated sugar to a simmer, then stir until the sugar is dissolved. Pour the hot cream over the chocolate. Let stand, covered, for 5 minutes, then stir until smooth. Chill the chocolate topping mixture until thickened but still pourable, about 30 minutes.

● Pour the chocolate over the pumpkin layer and chill the pie until the chocolate is set, about 1 hour.

136

Chocolate Turtle Pie

CRUST
1¼ cups graham cracker crumbs
½ stick (¼ cup) unsalted butter, melted
2 tablespoons granulated sugar
3 ounces milk chocolate, finely chopped

FILLING
¾ cup granulated sugar
3 tablespoons water

2 cups heavy cream, scalded
5 large egg yolks
6 ounces semisweet chocolate, finely chopped
1 teaspoon vanilla extract
¼ cup chopped pecans
¼ cup semisweet chocolate chips

Yield: One 9-inch pie

● Preheat the oven to 350°F.

● Make the crust: In a medium bowl, blend the graham cracker crumbs, butter, and sugar. Stir in the milk chocolate. Press the crust mixture into the bottom and up the sides of a 9-inch pie plate. Refrigerate until ready to use.

● Prepare the filling: In a heavy, medium saucepan, dissolve the sugar in the water over low heat, stirring constantly. Bring to a boil over medium-high heat, then let boil without stirring until the syrup turns a light amber. While the syrup is boiling, brush down the sides of the pan from time to time with a wet pastry brush to prevent crystals from forming. Remove the pan from the heat and stir in the hot cream (be careful, it will bubble rapidly). Continue stirring, over heat if necessary, until all of the caramel is dissolved into the cream.

● In a medium bowl, lightly beat the egg yolks. Whisk about ½ cup of the hot caramel cream into the eggs to warm them. Transfer the warmed eggs to the caramel cream in the saucepan. Stir in the chopped semisweet chocolate and the vanilla, stirring until melted and smooth.

● Pour the filling mixture into the pie crust. Sprinkle the pecans and chocolate chips on top. Bake for about 35 minutes, or until the center is just set. Transfer to a wire rack to cool completely, then refrigerate until firm, about 4 hours.

137

Milk Chocolate Toffee Cream Pie

CRUST

1½ cups chocolate wafer crumbs

5 tablespoons (¼ cup plus 1 tablespoon)
  unsalted butter, melted

2 tablespoons granulated sugar

FILLING

6 ounces milk chocolate, coarsely chopped

¾ cup heavy cream

8 ounces cream cheese, softened

¼ cup (packed) light brown sugar

1 tablespoon vanilla extract

¾ cup chopped chocolate-covered toffee candy

Yield: One 9-inch pie

- Preheat the oven to 350°F.

- Make the crust: In a medium bowl, combine the wafer crumbs, butter, and sugar. Press the mixture into the bottom and up the sides of a 9-inch pie plate. Bake for 10 minutes. Place on a wire rack to cool.

- Prepare the filling: Place the chocolate in a small bowl. In a small saucepan, bring ½ cup of the cream to a simmer. Pour the hot cream over the chocolate. Let stand, covered, for 5 minutes, then stir until smooth.

- In a medium bowl with an electric mixer, beat the cream cheese, sugar, and vanilla until smooth. Beat in the remaining ¼ cup cream. Gently beat in the cooled chocolate mixture. Fold in ½ cup of the chopped toffee candy.

- Pour the filling into the cooled crust, and sprinkle with the remaining ¼ cup of chopped toffee. Chill until firm, about 2 hours.

Use your fingers to shape a layer of the wafer crumb mixture over the bottom and sides of a 9-inch pie plate.

Rum-Soaked Chocolate Malibu

RUM SYRUP
½ cup granulated sugar
½ cup minced pitted prunes
¼ cup water
¼ cup dark rum
2 teaspoons instant coffee granules

CAKE
1¾ cups all-purpose flour
½ cup unsweetened cocoa powder
¾ teaspoon baking soda
¼ teaspoon baking powder
¼ teaspoon salt
1 stick (½ cup) unsalted butter

2 cups granulated sugar
3 large eggs
2 teaspoons vanilla extract
2 ounces unsweetened chocolate, melted
1⅓ cups buttermilk, at room temperature

CHOCOLATE GANACHE
16 ounces semisweet chocolate,
 finely chopped
2 cups heavy cream
2 tablespoons granulated sugar

Yield: 16 to 20 servings

• Prepare the rum syrup: In a small saucepan, combine the sugar, prunes, and water. Bring to a boil over medium heat, stirring constantly. Boil for 2 minutes. Remove from the heat and stir in the rum and coffee granules. Cover and set aside to steep.

• Make the cake: Preheat the oven to 350°F. Line an 11-by-17-inch jelly-roll pan with foil extending beyond the sides. Butter and flour the foil.

• In a medium bowl, whisk together the flour, cocoa, baking soda, baking powder, and salt. In a large bowl with an electric mixer, cream the butter and sugar. Beat in the eggs one at a time, beating well after each addition.

• Reserving the rum syrup, strain out the prunes and stir them into the batter along with the vanilla and melted chocolate. In three additions, alternately add the flour mixture and the buttermilk, beating well after each addition.

• Transfer the batter to the prepared pan and bake for 30 minutes, or until the center is set. Cool in the pan on a rack for 20 minutes. Then invert onto a rack,

remove the foil, and cool to room temperature, about 1 hour.

• Meanwhile, make the chocolate ganache: Place the chocolate in a medium bowl. In a medium saucepan, bring the cream to a simmer. Add the sugar and stir to dissolve. Pour the hot cream over the chocolate. Let stand for 5 minutes, then stir until smooth. Quick-chill in the refrigerator for about 45 minutes, then let sit at room temperature to reach a spreadable consistency.

• To assemble: Trimming off the outer edges, cut the cake crosswise into three 5-by-10-inch pieces. Cut out a piece of cardboard the same size and place a cake piece on the cardboard (this is the bottom layer). Prick the surface of all three pieces of cake with a toothpick. Brush the cake with the reserved rum syrup. Spread the bottom layer with ¾ cup of the chocolate ganache. Top with a second layer. Spread the second layer with another ¾ cup of chocolate ganache. Top with the last layer and frost the tops and sides with the remaining chocolate ganache. Chill in the refrigerator for 30 minutes to set.

Chocolate Torte with Raspberry Sauce

TORTE
2½ sticks (1¼ cups) unsalted butter
20 ounces semisweet chocolate,
 finely chopped
1 tablespoon vanilla extract or coffee liqueur
6 large eggs, at room temperature

GLAZE
⅓ cup heavy cream
⅓ cup semisweet chocolate chips

RASPBERRY SAUCE
Two 12-ounce packages unsweetened frozen
 raspberries
½ cup granulated sugar
2 tablespoons orange juice
Whipped cream, fresh raspberries, and
 Chocolate Leaves (page 230), for garnish

Yield: One 8½-inch torte

- Preheat the oven to 400°F. Butter the bottom and sides of an 8½-inch springform pan. Wrap the pan tightly in 2 layers of aluminum foil to keep the pan dry in the water bath. Place the springform in a large roasting pan and set aside.

- Make the torte: In a double boiler, melt the butter and chocolate. Stir until smooth. Remove from the heat and stir in the vanilla or coffee liqueur.

- In a medium bowl, beat the eggs. Set the bowl over a pan of simmering water and whisk the eggs until they are warm, about 3 minutes. Remove from the heat and beat the eggs with an electric mixer at high speed until light and tripled in volume, 4 to 5 minutes.

- Transfer the chocolate mixture to a large bowl and add one-fourth of the eggs. Mix thoroughly to lighten the chocolate. Gently fold the remaining

eggs into the chocolate mixture. Transfer immediately to the prepared springform. Pour hot water into the roasting pan until it reaches halfway up the sides of the springform.

- Bake for 18 minutes; the center will still be jiggly when removed from oven. Remove from the water bath and cool to room temperature, about 45 minutes. Remove the foil.

- Meanwhile, make the glaze: In a small saucepan, bring the cream to a simmer. Remove from the heat and add the chocolate chips. Cover for 15 minutes, then stir the mixture until smooth. Let cool to room temperature. Pour the glaze over the torte, then chill the torte in the refrigerator until firm, 6 to 8 hours.

- Prepare the sauce: Drain the berries in a fine-mesh sieve set over a bowl; press gently on the berries to remove as much juice as possible. Transfer the juice to a small saucepan and reduce to about ⅓ cup. Return the reduced juice to the bowl and stir in the sugar and orange juice. With a wooden spoon, press the raspberries through the strainer into the bowl. Stir to combine the purée with the juice.

• Run a knife around the edge of the torte to loosen it, then remove the sides of the springform pan. Serve the chilled torte with the raspberry sauce. Garnish with whipped cream, fresh raspberries, and Chocolate Leaves.

After gently warming eggs over simmering water, beat them with an electric mixer until they are tripled in volume and cool to the touch.

Far left, pour hot water into the roasting pan to come halfway up the sides of the springform pan. Near left, before pouring on the glaze, use a knife to loosen the edges of the torte from the springform so that when the pan is removed later it will not stick to the glaze.

Creamy Chocolate Fantasy

PASTRY
1½ cups all purpose flour
2 tablespoons granulated sugar
1 stick (½ cup) salted butter, chilled and cut
  into 8 pieces
5 to 6 tablespoons ice water

CUSTARD FILLING
1½ cups light cream
One 1½-inch vanilla bean split in half lengthwise or 2 teaspoons vanilla extract

4 large egg yolks
½ cup granulated sugar
2 tablespoons corn starch
1 cup (6 ounces) semisweet chocolate chips

MERINGUE
3 large egg whites
½ teaspoon cream of tartar
⅓ cup powdered sugar

Yield: 3 dozen tartlets

- To make pastry: In a medium bowl combine flour, sugar and butter with a pastry cutter until dough resembles coarse meal. Add water, and mix with a fork just until dough can be shaped into a ball.

- Wrap dough tightly in plastic wrap or a plastic bag. Refrigerate 1 hour or until firm.

- To make custard filling: In a medium saucepan scald cream with vanilla bean.

- In a small bowl lightly beat yolks with cornstarch until no lumps remain. Add sugar, then slowly whisk in 1 cup of the hot cream. Pour yolk-cream

back into the saucepan, and cook over medium-low heat, stirring constantly until mixture thickens enough to coat the back of a spoon. Do not boil or egg will curdle.

- Transfer custard into a medium bowl, and stir in chocolate chips until melted. If you're using vanilla extract, stir it in with the chocolate chips. Wrap custard tightly and refrigerate.

- To make meringue: In a medium bowl with an electric mixer on high speed, beat egg whites until foamy. Add cream of tartar and half the sugar; beat until thickened. Gradually add the remaining sugar, beating continuously on high just until stiff peaks form. Do not overbeat or peaks may fall.

- Preheat oven to 400°F.

- To assemble: On floured surface with a floured rolling pin, roll out dough to ¼-inch thickness. Use a cookie cutter or a drinking glass 2 inches in diameter to cut out rounds of dough. Lightly press pastry into miniature muffin or pastry cups.

- Refrigerate for 15 minutes. Then prick bottom and sides of each pastry cup with a fork. Bake for 10 to 12 minutes or until edges turn golden brown. Cool pastry to room temperature.

- Spoon (or pipe with a pastry bag) 1 tablespoon of cooled chocolate custard into each pastry cup and top with meringue.

- Reduce oven temperature to 350°F. Bake pastries for 6 to 8 minutes, or until meringue begins to turn light golden brown. Cool and serve.

Use a pastry bag with a medium plain or star tip to pipe a tablespoon of chocolate custard into each pastry cup (left). Top with a swirl of meringue, covering the custard completely (below).

Chocolate Pudding Soufflé Cake

CAKE

½ stick (¼ cup) unsalted butter
3 ounces unsweetened chocolate
½ cup cake flour
½ teaspoon baking powder
¼ teaspoon salt
6 large eggs—3 separated, 3 whole
1 cup granulated sugar
¼ teaspoon cream of tartar

PUDDING

5 large egg yolks
½ cup granulated sugar
2 tablespoons cornstarch
2½ cups heavy cream
8 ounces semisweet chocolate, finely chopped
2 teaspoons vanilla extract

Yield: One 9-inch layer cake

- Preheat the oven to 375°F. Grease a 9-inch spring-form pan.

- Make the cake: In a double boiler, melt the butter and unsweetened chocolate. Stir until smooth, then set aside. In a small bowl, combine the flour, baking powder, and salt. In a large bowl with an electric mixer, beat the 3 whole eggs and 3 egg yolks with ¾ cup of the sugar until pale and lemon-colored. Slowly beat in the chocolate mixture. Then beat in the flour mixture.

- In a medium bowl, beat the egg whites until foamy. Add the cream of tartar and beat until soft peaks form. Beat in the remaining ¼ cup sugar until stiff glossy peaks form. Stir one-third of the egg whites into the batter to lighten it. Gently and thoroughly fold in the remaining whites. Transfer the batter to the prepared pan and smooth the top.

- Bake for 40 to 50 minutes, or until the center is set. Transfer to a wire rack to cool to room temperature. Refrigerate until firm.

- Meanwhile, make the pudding: In a medium bowl, lightly beat the egg yolks. In a heavy medium saucepan, whisk together the sugar and cornstarch. Gradually whisk in the cream. Bring the mixture to a boil over low heat, whisking constantly.

- Very gradually whisk the hot cream into the egg yolks, then return the mixture to the saucepan and cook over very low heat, whisking constantly, until the pudding is very thick and steamy; do not let it boil. Remove the pudding from the heat, stir in the chocolate and vanilla, and stir until melted and smooth. Transfer the pudding to a bowl, place a piece of plastic wrap directly on the surface, and refrigerate until cold, at least 2 hours.

- To assemble: Remove the sides of the springform. With a long serrated knife, cut the cake horizontally into 3 even layers. Place one layer on a serving plate. Spread about ¾ cup of pudding on top. Top with a second layer and spread with another ¾ cup of pudding. Top with the third layer and spread the tops and sides with the remaining pudding. Refrigerate until set.

Lemon-Glazed Pound Cake

CAKE
3 cups cake flour, sifted
2 cups granulated sugar
½ teaspoon salt
1 teaspoon baking powder
3 sticks (1½ cups) salted butter, softened
⅓ cup buttermilk, at room temperature
6 large eggs
2 teaspoons lemon extract
1 tablespoon grated lemon zest
  (2 medium lemons)

GLAZE
¼ cup freshly squeezed lemon juice
¼ cup granulated sugar

TOPPING
2 tablespoons powdered sugar, sifted

Yield: 2 dozen slices

- Preheat oven to 350°F. Grease and flour a 3-quart fluted tube pan or bundt pan.

- In a large bowl with an electric mixer on low speed, blend flour, sugar, salt and baking powder. Add butter, buttermilk and 3 eggs. Beat on low until dry ingredients are moistened. Increase speed to high and beat for 2 minutes. Scrape down sides of bowl.

- Add lemon extract and lemon zest, and blend at medium speed. Add the remaining 3 eggs one at a time, beating at high speed for 30 seconds after each addition.

- Pour batter into prepared pan, and bake for 50 to 60 minutes or until a toothpick inserted into cake comes out clean.

- While pound cake is baking, prepare lemon glaze. In a small saucepan heat lemon juice and sugar over low heat. Stir constantly until sugar dissolves.

- When cake is done, remove from oven and leave cake in pan. With a toothpick, poke holes in the surface of the cake, and pour half the glaze over it.

- Cool in pan 15 minutes, then invert on cooling rack. Brush top of pound cake with remaining lemon glaze. Cool to room temperature, then dust with powdered sugar.

With a toothpick, poke holes in the surface of the cake (top). Then pour the lemon glaze over the holes, letting it drizzle into the cake (bottom). Saturating this pound cake with lemon is the secret to its moistness.

Poppy Seed Bundt Cake

3 cups cake flour, sifted
2 cups granulated sugar
½ teaspoon salt
1 teaspoon baking powder
3 sticks (1½ cups) salted butter, softened
½ cup (4 ounces) sour cream
6 large eggs

⅓ cup cream sherry
⅓ cup poppy seeds

TOPPING
¼ cup powdered sugar

Yield: 24 servings

- Preheat oven to 350°F. Grease and flour a 3-quart fluted tube pan or bundt pan.

- In large bowl with an electric mixer blend flour, sugar, salt and baking powder on low until all ingredients are distributed equally. Add butter, sour cream and 3 of the eggs, and mix on medium until the dry ingredients are moistened. Beat on high for 2 minutes, then scrape bowl.

- Add remaining 3 eggs, one at a time, alternating with the sherry. Beat well after each addition. Blend in poppy seeds on low speed.

- Pour batter into prepared pan and bake for 50 to 60 minutes or until toothpick inserted into the center of cake comes out clean. Cool in pan 10 minutes, then invert cake onto a rack to cool. When cake has cooled completely, lightly dust top with powdered sugar.

Mocha Mousse Cheesecake

CRUST
4 ounces chocolate chip cookie crumbs
  (about 1 cup)
2 tablespoons salted butter, melted

FILLING
24 ounces cream cheese, softened
½ cup granulated sugar
½ cup (packed) light brown sugar
8 ounces sour cream (about 1 cup)
3 large eggs

7 ounces semisweet chocolate chips,
  melted (about 1¼ cups)
½ cup coffee, freshly brewed
1 tablespoon vanilla extract

GLAZE
5 ounces semisweet chocolate
  (about ¾ cup)
½ stick (¼ cup) salted butter, softened

Yield: 12 to 16 servings

- Preheat oven to 350°F.

- Make the crust: Use a blender or a food processor with a metal blade to grind cookies into fine crumbs. Add butter and blend until smooth. Press crust into bottom of a 9-inch springform pan. Refrigerate while preparing mousse.

- Make the filling: In a large bowl with an electric mixer, beat the cream cheese until very smooth. Add sugars and sour cream, and blend thoroughly. Add eggs and beat until mixture is smooth.

- Add melted chocolate, coffee, and vanilla, again blending ingredients until smooth. Pour filling into prepared pan, and bake in middle of oven for 50 to 60 minutes.

- Turn off oven, crack door 1 inch, and leave cheesecake in oven 1 hour to set. Then remove from oven and cool to room temperature.

- Make the glaze: In a small saucepan melt chocolate and butter over low heat; stir until smooth. Pour glaze over top of cheesecake and smooth with a metal spatula. Refrigerate 3 to 4 hours or until firm. Cut and serve.

When baked cheesecake has cooled, pour chocolate-butter glaze over the top, and smooth with a metal spatula to form a thin chocolate frosting.

Carrot Cake

CAKE
2½ cups all-purpose flour
2 teaspoons baking soda
¼ teaspoon salt
2 teaspoons cinnamon
1 cup light brown sugar, packed
1 cup granulated sugar
3 sticks (1½ cups) salted butter, softened
3 large eggs
2 teaspoons vanilla extract
3 cups grated carrot (3 to 4 medium carrots)
½ cup crushed pineapple, drained

1 cup (6 ounces) raisins
1 cup (4 ounces) chopped walnuts

ICING
16 ounces cream cheese, softened
1 stick (½ cup) salted butter, softened
1 tablespoon fresh lemon juice
  (about 1 large lemon)
2 teaspoons vanilla extract
3 cups powdered sugar

Yield: 12 to 16 servings

- Preheat oven to 350°F. Grease and flour two 9-inch cake pans.

- In a large bowl stir together flour, baking soda, salt, cinnamon and sugars. Add butter, one egg and vanilla; blend with electric mixer on low speed. Increase speed to medium and beat for 2 minutes.

- Scrape down sides of bowl. Add remaining eggs, one at a time, beating 30 seconds after each addition. Add carrots, pineapple, raisins and walnuts. Blend on low until thoroughly combined.

- Pour batter into prepared pans and smooth the surface with a rubber spatula. Bake in center of oven for 60 to 70 minutes. Toothpick inserted into center should come out clean. Cool in pans for 10 minutes. Then invert cakes on rack and cool to room temperature.

- To prepare icing: On a medium bowl with electric mixer on medium speed, beat cream cheese and butter until smooth. Add lemon juice and vanilla; beat until combined. Add sugar gradually, mixing on low until smooth.

- To ice the carrot cake: Place one layer on a cake platter, and with a metal spatula spread icing over the top to form a thin filling. Place second layer over the first, rounded side up. Coat the top and sides of the cake evenly with remaining icing. Refrigerate for 1 hour to set icing.

With a metal spatula, spread icing over bottom cake layer to form a thin filling. Top with second cake layer, and ice the surface and sides evenly. For an elegant finish, pipe on a border with a pastry bag and a medium star tip.

Chocolate Waffle Pillows

WAFFLES

2 cups all-purpose flour
1 teaspoon baking powder
1 cup unsweetened cocoa powder
2 sticks (1 cup) salted butter, softened
2 cups granulated sugar
5 large eggs
2 teaspoons vanilla extract

TOPPINGS

⅓ cup powdered sugar
⅓ cup unsweetened cocoa powder
1 cup fresh raspberries
1 pint whipping cream, whipped
½ cup chocolate syrup

Yield: About 3½ dozen

- Grease and preheat waffle iron.

- In medium bowl combine flour, baking powder and cocoa. Mix well with a wire whisk. Set aside.

- In large bowl with an electric mixer cream butter and sugar. Add eggs and vanilla and beat at medium speed. Batter will appear slightly curdled. Scrape down the sides of the bowl, then add the flour mixture and blend on low speed until just combined. Do not overmix.

- Drop by rounded tablespoons onto hot waffle iron, using about one tablespoon per 4-by-4-inch square. Cook approximately 1 minute. Carefully transfer to cool surface.

- Use any of the following toppings singly or in combination: a dusting of powdered sugar and cocoa powder; fresh raspberries and whipped cream; a drizzle of chocolate syrup.

Chocolate Macadamia Cream Satin

CAKE
1 cup all-purpose flour
1½ teaspoons baking soda
1 teaspoon salt
¾ cup light brown sugar, packed
¾ cup granulated sugar
1 stick (½ cup) salted butter, softened
¼ cup unsweetened cocoa powder
¼ cup boiling water
2 large eggs, beaten
1 teaspoon vanilla extract
1 cup buttermilk

FILLING
¼ cup granulated sugar
14 ounces cream cheese, at room temperature

1 large egg
1 pound white chocolate bar
2½ teaspoons (1 package) unflavored gelatin
2 tablespoons cold water
1 cup (½ pint) whipping cream
3 tablespoons vanilla extract

DECORATIONS
4 cups (24 ounces) unsalted macadamia nuts
¼ cup cocoa powder
¼ cup powdered sugar
½ cup (¼ pint) whipping cream (optional)
1 ounce dark or white chocolate (optional)

Yield: 12 servings

● Preheat oven to 350°F. Grease and flour an 8- or 9-inch springform pan.

● In a medium bowl combine flour, baking soda, and salt. Mix well with a wire whisk and set aside.

● In a large bowl combine sugars with an electric mixer on medium speed. Add butter and beat to form a grainy paste.

● In a small bowl combine cocoa powder and boiling water, and stir until smooth. Add cocoa mixture, eggs and vanilla to butter and sugar; blend well to form a smooth batter. Alternately add the flour mixture and the buttermilk to the batter. Blend at low speed just until combined.

● Pour into prepared pan. Bake for 25 to 35 minutes or until a knife inserted into middle of the cake comes out clean. Leaving cake in pan, cool to room temperature, then refrigerate to make slicing easier.

- To prepare the filling: In a medium bowl with an electric mixer and clean beaters, beat sugar and cream cheese until well blended. Add egg and beat until light and fluffy.

- Next melt white chocolate in a double boiler. While chocolate is melting, in a small metal bowl sprinkle gelatin over the cold water. Let gelatin bloom for 5 minutes, then dissolve it over a double boiler until clear and smooth.

- Gradually add dissolved gelatin to the cream cheese-sugar mixture, beating continuously at medium speed until smooth. (If you beat it too fast, the gelatin will stick to the sides of the bowl.)

- Add whipped cream to the mixture and blend until smooth. With a rubber spatula, fold the white chocolate and vanilla into the cake batter thoroughly.

- To assemble cake and filling: Remove sides of springform pan. Cut cake into 2 thin layers and set the top layer aside. Replace sides of the springform pan, leaving bottom layer of cake in pan.

- Pour filling over bottom cake layer. Carefully place the other cake layer on top of the filling. Refrigerate for several hours.

- When filling is firm, remove sides of pan and place the cake on a platter. Coat the sides of the cake with macadamia nuts. Dust the top of the cake with a mixture of cocoa powder and powdered sugar. If desired, add rosettes of whipped cream, chocolate shavings and more macadamia nuts. Refrigerate until ready to serve.

Using a bread knife, carefully cut cake into two thin layers (top). Return bottom layer to springform pan, and pour the filling on top (center, right). Finally, cap the filling with the top layer (bottom, right).

Chocolate Swirl Banana Cake

2¼ cups all-purpose flour
1 teaspoon baking soda
1¼ cups light brown sugar, firmly packed
½ stick (¼ cup) salted butter
½ cup sour cream
1½ cups mashed banana
  (about 3 large bananas)
1 large egg
1 teaspoon vanilla extract

¾ cup (4½ ounces) semisweet chocolate
  chips, melted

GANACHE
½ cup heavy cream
⅔ cup (4 ounces) semisweet chocolate,
  finely chopped

Yield: 16 servings

- Preheat oven to 350°F. Grease an 8-by-8-inch baking pan.

- In medium bowl combine flour and soda. Mix well with a wire whisk. Set aside.

- Blend sugar and butter in a large bowl using an electric mixer. Scrape sides of bowl. Add sour cream, banana, egg and vanilla, and beat at medium speed until smooth. Add the flour mixture and blend at low speed until just combined. Do not overmix. Gently fold in melted chocolate and stir just until marbled pattern develops.

- Pour batter into the prepared pan. Bake for 40 to 45 minutes or until toothpick inserted into center comes out clean. Cool in pan 15 minutes, then invert onto rack and cool to room temperature.

- To prepare the ganache: Scald cream in a small saucepan. Remove from heat and add chocolate. Cover pan with lid and set aside. After about 15 minutes, stir frosting until it is smooth. Transfer to bowl and refrigerate until firm, about 30 minutes. Turn cake right side up onto a serving plate and frost liberally with the ganache.

Pour the melted chocolate directly into the cake batter (far left). Stir the chocolate into the batter only until a swirled, marbled pattern forms (left). The cake will show the swirl when baked.

Mocha Pudding Cake

CAKE

1 ounce unsweetened chocolate,
    finely chopped
1 tablespoon unsalted butter
1 cup all-purpose flour
⅔ cup granulated sugar
1 teaspoon instant espresso granules
½ teaspoon baking powder
½ teaspoon baking soda
¼ teaspoon salt
½ cup milk

SAUCE

⅔ cup (packed) light brown sugar
½ stick (¼ cup) unsalted butter
2 ounces unsweetened chocolate,
    finely chopped
⅛ teaspoon salt
1 cup very hot, freshly brewed coffee
1 tablespoon coffee liqueur
Coffee ice cream, for serving

Yield: 6 servings

- Preheat the oven to 350°F. Lightly butter six 6-ounce custard cups.

- Make the cakes: In a double boiler, melt the chocolate and the butter. Set aside to cool slightly.

- In a medium bowl, combine the flour, granulated sugar, espresso granules, baking powder, baking soda, and salt. Gradually blend in the melted chocolate mixture and the milk. Dividing evenly, pour the batter into the prepared custard cups.

- For the sauce: Place the brown sugar, butter, chocolate, and salt in a medium bowl. Pour the hot coffee over the chocolate mixture and let stand for 1 minute. Add the coffee liqueur and whisk until the chocolate and butter are melted and the mixture is smooth.

- Dividing evenly, spoon the pudding sauce over the cake batter; do not stir. Bake for 30 minutes, or until the cakes are just firm to the touch. (The bot-

tom of the cakes, where the sauce ends up, will stay very liquid.)

- Let the cakes stand for 10 to 15 minutes. Invert the cakes onto dessert plates, making sure to get all of the sauce. Serve warm with a scoop of coffee ice cream.

Spoon the pudding sauce on top of the cake batter in the custard cups. Do not stir. The sauce will sink to the bottom of the cups as the pudding cakes bake.

153

Glazed Five-Layer Ice Cream Cake

CAKE

1 ounce unsweetened chocolate
¾ cup sifted cake flour
1 teaspoon baking soda
¼ teaspoon salt
3 tablespoons unsalted butter
¾ cup (packed) light brown sugar
1 large egg
½ teaspoon vanilla extract
⅓ cup sour cream
⅓ cup boiling water

FUDGE SAUCE

4 ounces semisweet chocolate,
  coarsely chopped
5 tablespoons unsalted butter
¼ cup unsweetened cocoa powder
½ cup water

¼ cup heavy cream
¾ cup granulated sugar
¼ cup light corn syrup
2 teaspoons vanilla extract

CHOCOLATE MERINGUE

2 large egg whites, at room temperature
¼ cup granulated sugar
1 tablespoon unsweetened cocoa powder

ASSEMBLY AND GLAZE

1½ cups coffee ice cream, softened
½ cup heavy cream
4 ounces semisweet chocolate chips
Whipped cream, for garnish

Yield: 12 servings

- Preheat the oven to 350°F.

- Make the cake: Butter and flour an 8½-inch spring-form pan.

- In a double boiler, melt the chocolate over hot, not simmering, water. Set aside to cool slightly.

- In a small bowl, whisk together the flour, baking soda, and salt.

- In a medium bowl with an electric mixer, cream the butter and brown sugar. Beat in the egg and vanilla. Beat in the melted chocolate. Beat in the

flour mixture. Beat in the sour cream and boiling water.

- Scrape the batter into the prepared pan and bake for 20 minutes, or until the center springs back when lightly pressed. Cool in the pan on a rack for 15 minutes, then invert the cake onto the rack to cool completely.

- Prepare the fudge sauce: In a heavy medium saucepan, stir together the chocolate, butter, cocoa, water, and cream. Bring the sauce to a simmer over low heat and stir in the granulated sugar and corn syrup. Simmer until the sauce is quite thick but still pourable, 5 to 6 minutes. Remove from the heat and stir in the vanilla. Let the fudge sauce cool to room temperature.

● Make the meringue: Preheat the oven to 250°F. In a medium bowl, beat the egg whites until foamy. Add the granulated sugar gradually, beating until stiff peaks form. Gently fold in the cocoa. Using an 8-inch cake pan as a guide, draw a circle on a sheet of parchment paper or wax paper and set on a baking sheet. Grease the paper lightly and smooth the meringue very evenly inside the circle. Bake for 2 hours. Turn the oven off, open the door a crack, and leave the meringue in the oven for 1 hour.

● To assemble: With a long serrated knife, slice the cake layer horizontally into two even layers. Place one layer in the bottom of an 8½-inch springform pan. Pour half of the fudge sauce on top and place in the freezer for 15 minutes to set.

● In a medium bowl, beat the softened ice cream with a wooden spoon until smooth. Spread the ice cream over the fudge sauce and smooth the top. Top with the remaining cake layer and remaining fudge sauce. Top the cake with the meringue layer and return to the freezer while you make the glaze..

● Make the glaze: In a small saucepan, bring the cream to a boil. Remove from the heat, add the chocolate chips, cover, and set aside for 15 minutes. Stir until smooth. Quickly pour the glaze over the meringue, tilting the springform pan to evenly coat the top. Cover the springform with foil and freeze for 6 to 8 hours or overnight.

● To serve: Wrap a hot, wet towel around the sides of the pan for 5 minutes. Run a thin sharp knife around the edges of the pan to loosen the cake; remove the sides. Serve wedges of the cake garnished with whipped cream rosettes.

Using a cake pan as a guide, draw an 8-inch circle on a sheet of parchment or wax paper. Spread the chocolate meringue evenly inside the circle.

Far left, using toothpicks to mark the cutting line, use a long serrated knife to cut the cake horizontally into two even layers. Near left, top the layers of cake, ice cream, and fudge sauce with the baked meringue circle.

Chocolate Chip Cheesecake

CRUST
5 ounces chocolate cookie crumbs
  (about 1 cup)
2 tablespoons salted butter, softened

FILLING
16 ounces cream cheese, softened
1 cup granulated sugar
16 ounces sour cream (about 2 cups)
3 large eggs
1 tablespoon vanilla extract
9 ounces semisweet chocolate chips,
  divided (about 1½ cups)

Yield: 12 to 16 servings

- Preheat oven to 350°F.

- Prepare the crust: Grind cookies into fine crumbs using a blender or a food processor fitted with a metal blade. Add butter and blend until smooth. Press crust into bottom of 9-inch springform pan, and refrigerate while preparing the filling.

- Prepare the filling: Beat cream cheese until smooth in a large bowl using an electric mixer. Blend in sugar and sour cream. Add the eggs and vanilla, and mix until smooth.

- Using a wooden spoon, stir in 1 cup of the chocolate chips. Pour filling into the crust-lined pan, and smooth top with a spatula. Sprinkle the remaining ½ cup chocolate chips evenly over the top. Bake 30 to 40 minutes. Turn oven off and leave cheesecake in oven for 1 hour to set. Remove from oven and chill in refrigerator until firm, about 3 to 4 hours.

White Ivory Cream Cake

CAKE

8 ounces white chocolate, finely chopped
3 cups sifted cake flour
2 teaspoons baking powder
½ teaspoon salt
1 stick (½ cup) unsalted butter
1¼ cups granulated sugar
3 large eggs
2 teaspoons vanilla extract
1 cup plus 1 tablespoon milk

FILLING AND FROSTING

1½ pounds white chocolate, finely chopped
2½ cups heavy cream
6 tablespoons unsalted butter
½ cup coarsely chopped macadamia nuts
Whole macadamia nuts and strawberries,
 for garnish

Yield: One 9-inch layer cake

- Preheat the oven to 350°F. Butter and flour two 9-inch cake pans.

- Make the cake: In a double boiler, melt the white chocolate over hot, not simmering, water. Set aside to cool slightly.

- In a medium bowl, whisk together the flour, baking powder, and salt.

- In a large bowl with an electric mixer, cream the butter and sugar. Beat in the eggs one at a time, beating well after each addition. On low speed, beat in the melted chocolate and the vanilla. In three additions, on low speed, alternately beat in the flour mixture and the milk. Beat until just smooth, about 20 seconds.

- Pour the batter into the prepared pans and bake for 25 to 30 minutes, or until the top is golden and a cake tester inserted in the center comes out clean. Set the cake pans on a wire rack to cool for 20 minutes. Then invert the cakes onto the racks to cool

the layers completely.

- Prepare the filling and frosting: Place the white chocolate in a medium bowl. In a small heavy saucepan, bring 1½ cups of the cream and the butter to a simmer. Pour over the chocolate. Let stand, covered, for 5 minutes, then stir until smooth. Refrigerate the white chocolate mixture until firm enough to spread, about 1 hour.

- To assemble: Spread the bottom layer with 1 cup of the chilled white chocolate mixture. Arrange the chopped macadamia nuts over the filling. Top with the second cake layer.

- In a medium bowl, beat the remaining 1 cup cream until firm peaks form. Fold the whipped cream into the remaining white chocolate mixture. Spread this over the top and sides of the cake. Arrange whole macadamia nuts around the rim and base of the cake. Chill until ready to serve. Garnish each slice with a fanned whole strawberry.

Chocolate Carmalua

CAKE

3½ sticks (1¾ cups) unsalted butter
1¼ cups granulated sugar
2 tablespoons instant espresso granules,
  dissolved in 1 cup hot water
10 ounces semisweet or bittersweet chocolate,
  finely chopped
4 ounces unsweetened chocolate,
  finely chopped
6 large eggs
6 large egg yolks
2 teaspoons vanilla extract

CHOCOLATE CARAMEL GLAZE

½ cup granulated sugar
3 tablespoons water
½ cup heavy cream, scalded
½ stick (¼ cup) unsalted butter,
  softened
2 ounces semisweet chocolate, chopped
1 tablespoon coffee liqueur
Powdered sugar, for garnish

Yield: 12 to 16 servings

• Preheat the oven to 325°F. Butter an 8½-inch springform pan and wrap the pan tightly with aluminum foil.

• Make the cake: In a heavy medium saucepan, combine the butter, granulated sugar, and coffee mixture. Cook over medium-low heat, stirring frequently, until the sugar is dissolved, about 10 minutes. Add the semisweet and unsweetened chocolates and stir until melted and smooth. Remove the pan from the heat.

• In a large bowl, whisk together the eggs and egg yolks. Whisk in the chocolate mixture and vanilla until well blended. Pour the batter into the prepared pan. Place the pan on a baking sheet and bake for 55 minutes, or until the edges crack slightly but the center is not completely set. Set the pan on a wire rack to cool completely. (The cake will sink as it cools.)

• Prepare the chocolate caramel glaze: In a small heavy saucepan, dissolve the sugar in the water over low heat, stirring constantly. Bring to a boil over medium-high heat, then let boil without stirring until the syrup turns a deep amber color. While the syrup is boiling, brush down the sides of the pan from time to time with a wet pastry brush to prevent crystals from forming. Remove the pan from the heat and stir in the hot cream (be careful, it will bubble rapidly). Continue stirring, over low heat if necessary, until the caramel is dissolved into the cream. Add the butter and chocolate, and stir until smooth. Stir in the coffee liqueur. Cool to room temperature. Pour the glaze over the cooled cake, cover the springform with plastic wrap, and chill for 4 to 6 hours.

• Run a knife around the edge of the cake to loosen it from the sides of the springform and remove the sides of the pan. Transfer the cake to a serving plate and dust with powdered sugar in a decorative pattern, if desired.

Swiss Chocolate Cheesecake

CRUST

1½ cups vanilla wafer crumbs
½ stick (¼ cup) unsalted butter, melted
½ cup finely ground toasted almonds

FILLING

16 ounces milk chocolate, finely chopped
1½ pounds cream cheese, softened
1 cup granulated sugar
¼ teaspoon salt
4 large eggs
½ cup light cream or half-and-half
2 teaspoons vanilla extract

CHOCOLATE GLAZE

2 ounces semisweet chocolate,
  coarsely chopped
3 tablespoons unsalted butter
¼ cup water
2 tablespoons unsweetened cocoa powder
2 tablespoons light corn syrup
⅓ cup granulated sugar
1 teaspoon vanilla extract
Milk chocolate curls, for garnish

Yield: One 9-inch cake

- Preheat the oven to 300°F.

- Make the crust: In a medium bowl, combine the cookie crumbs, butter, and almonds until well blended. Press the moistened crumbs into the bottom and 1½ inches up the sides of a 9-inch spring-form pan.

- Prepare the filling: In a double boiler, melt the milk chocolate over hot, not simmering, water. Set aside to cool slightly.

- In a large bowl with an electric mixer, beat the cream cheese until creamy. Add the sugar and salt and beat until blended. Beat in the eggs one at a time, beating well after each addition. Stir in the melted chocolate, cream, and vanilla until well blended.

- Pour the batter into the prepared crust and bake for 1 hour. Turn off the heat but leave the cheesecake in the oven for 1 hour. Remove from the oven and set on a wire rack to cool to room temperature.

- Meanwhile, make the chocolate glaze: In a small saucepan, combine the semisweet chocolate, butter, water, and cocoa. Stir over low heat until melted and smooth. Add the corn syrup and sugar, then stir until the sugar dissolves. Increase the heat and bring the sauce to a low boil, then cook until the sauce thickens, 12 to 15 minutes. Remove from the heat, stir in the vanilla, and set aside to cool to room temperature.

- Pour the cooled glaze over the room-temperature cheesecake. Chill until firm, 6 to 8 hours. Sprinkle the top with the milk chocolate curls.

Chocolate Fudge Layered Banana Cake

CAKE
2½ cups cake flour, sifted
2 teaspoons baking soda
½ teaspoon salt
1½ sticks (¾ cup) unsalted butter, softened
1¾ cups granulated sugar
4 large eggs
2½ cups mashed bananas
  plus 2 whole bananas
1 teaspoon vanilla extract
½ cup mini semisweet chocolate chips

GANACHE FILLING
½ cup heavy cream
¼ cup sour cream
9 ounces semisweet chocolate, finely chopped

CHOCOLATE GLAZE
½ cup heavy cream
1 tablespoon unsalted butter
6 ounces semisweet chocolate, finely chopped

Yield: 8 servings

- Preheat the oven to 350°F. Butter a 12-by-17-inch jelly-roll pan. Line the pan with parchment or wax paper, then butter and flour the paper.

- Make the cake: In a small bowl, whisk together the flour, baking soda, and salt.

- In a large bowl with an electric mixer, cream the butter and sugar. Add the eggs one at a time, beating well after each addition. Beat in the mashed bananas and the vanilla. Beat in the flour mixture and the chocolate chips until smooth. Pour the batter into the prepared pan and bake for 20 to 25 minutes, or until the center is set. Cool on a rack to room temperature.

- Loosen the cake with a spatula and carefully invert onto a large piece of foil. Cut the cake lengthwise into two pieces 5 by 15 inches, trimming off the outside edges of the cake.

- Prepare the ganache filling: In a heavy medium saucepan, bring the cream to a simmer. Remove from the heat and stir in the sour cream. Pour the mixture over the chocolate in a medium bowl, then stir until smooth. Refrigerate until the filling firms up but is still spreadable

- In a medium bowl, combine flour, soda, and salt. Mix well with wire whisk. Set aside.

- Spread the ganache filling over one cake layer. Slice the 2 whole bananas into ¼-inch slices and arrange evenly over the ganache. Place the second cake layer on top.

- Make the glaze: In a heavy medium saucepan, bring the cream to a simmer. Remove from the heat and stir in the butter and chocolate. Stir until smooth.

- Pour the warm glaze over the cake and smooth, allowing it to run down the sides. Place the cake in the freezer to firm for 30 to 40 minutes. Cut the cake crosswise into 8 slices and let sit at room temperature for 15 minutes before serving.

White Chocolate Cheesecake

CRUST
1½ cups ladyfinger crumbs
4 ounces white chocolate, coarsely chopped
5 tablespoons unsalted butter, melted

FILLING
18 ounces white chocolate
¼ cup heavy cream
1½ pounds cream cheese, softened
½ cup granulated sugar
½ cup sour cream

4 large eggs
1 tablespoon vanilla extract

WHITE CHOCOLATE GANACHE
8 ounces white chocolate, finely chopped
½ cup heavy cream
1 tablespoon unsalted butter
Fresh raspberries, for garnish
Raspberry Sauce (page 197)

Yield: 12 to 16 servings

- Make the crust: In a food processor or blender, combine the ladyfinger crumbs and the white chocolate and process until the chocolate is finely chopped. Blend in the butter. Wrap the outside of a 9-inch springform pan in aluminum foil. Press the crust into the bottom and up the sides of the pan. Chill the crust.

- Preheat the oven to 275°F. Set a shallow baking pan filled with hot water on the bottom rack of the oven.

- Prepare the filling: In a double boiler, melt the white chocolate with the cream over hot, not simmering, water. Set aside to cool slightly.

- In a large bowl, beat the cream cheese and sugar until smooth. Beat in the sour cream, eggs, and vanilla. Beat in the white chocolate cream. Pour into the prepared pan.

- Set the cheesecake on the center rack and bake for

1 hour. Reduce the heat to 250°F and bake for 1 more hour. Without opening the oven, turn off the heat but leave the cake in the oven for 1 hour. Cool the cheesecake on a rack for 30 minutes.

- Meanwhile, make the ganache: Place the white chocolate in a medium bowl. In a small saucepan, bring the cream and butter to a simmer. Pour the hot cream over the chocolate. Let stand, covered, for 5 minutes, then stir until smooth. Let the ganache cool to room temperature.

- Pour the ganache over the cheesecake and spread it smooth. Cover the cheesecake and refrigerate for at least 8 hours or overnight.

- To unmold, wrap a hot wet towel around the pan, then remove the sides of the springform. Garnish the cheesecake with fresh raspberries. Cut into wedges and serve with the Raspberry Sauce.

Chocolate-Toffee Speckled Cake

CAKE
3 cups sifted cake flour
1¼ teaspoons baking powder
½ teaspoon baking soda
½ teaspoon salt
1 stick (½ cup) unsalted butter, softened
1½ cups (packed) light brown sugar
¼ cup sour cream
6 large egg yolks
2 teaspoons vanilla extract

¾ cup plus 2 tablespoons milk, at
  room temperature
6 ounces semisweet chocolate, finely grated

CHOCOLATE GANACHE
18 ounces milk chocolate, finely chopped
1½ cups heavy cream
1 cup chopped chocolate-covered toffee

Yield: One 9-inch layer cake

- Preheat the oven to 350°F. Butter two 9-inch cake pans. Line the bottoms with circles of wax paper, then butter and flour the paper.

- Make the cake: In a medium bowl, whisk together the flour, baking powder, baking soda, and salt.

- In a medium bowl with an electric mixer, cream the butter and sugar. Beat in the sour cream. Beat in the yolks one at a time. Beat in the vanilla. In three additions, alternately stir in the flour mixture and the milk, beating well after each addition. Fold in the semisweet chocolate.

- Spread the batter in the prepared pans and bake for 30 to 35 minutes, or until a cake tester inserted in the center comes out clean. Cool the cakes in the pans on a rack for 20 minutes. Then invert the

cakes onto the racks to cool completely.

- Meanwhile, make the ganache: Place the milk chocolate in a medium bowl. In a small saucepan, bring the cream to a boil. Pour over the chocolate. Let stand, covered, for 5 minutes, then stir until smooth. Chill in the refrigerator for 1 hour.

- To assemble: With an electric mixer, slowly beat the ganache until thickened and smooth; be careful not to overbeat or the ganache will separate.

- Spread 1½ cups of the ganache over the bottom cake layer. Sprinkle with half of the chopped toffee. Top with the second cake layer. Frost with the remaining ganache. Sprinkle the top of the cake with the remaining toffee. Refrigerate the cake until ready to serve.

Black and White Cupcakes

CREAM CHEESE LAYER
8 ounces cream cheese, softened
¼ cup granulated sugar
1 large egg

CAKE LAYER
1½ cups all-purpose flour
1 cup granulated sugar
¼ cup plus 1 tablespoon unsweetened
  cocoa powder

1 teaspoon baking soda
½ teaspoon salt
½ cup water
⅓ cup vegetable oil
1 large egg
1 teaspoon vanilla extract
3 ounces semisweet chocolate
  chips (½ cup)

Yield: 12 cupcakes

- Preheat the oven to 350°F. Line 12 muffin cups with foil or paper muffin cup liners.

- Prepare the cream cheese layer: In a medium bowl, beat the cream cheese until smooth. Beat in the sugar and egg until well blended.

- Make the cake layer: In a large bowl, whisk together the flour, sugar, cocoa, baking soda, and salt. In a small bowl, beat the water, oil, egg, and vanilla. Add to the flour mixture and stir until just combined. Stir in half of the chocolate chips.

- Fill the muffin cups about half full with the chocolate cake batter. Using the remaining cake batter and all of the cream cheese batter, spoon equal amounts on top of the cake batter, creating a top that is half chocolate and half cream cheese. Sprinkle the tops of the cupcakes with the remaining chocolate chips.

- Bake for 30 to 35 minutes, or until a cake tester inserted into the center comes out clean. Set the muffin tin on a wire rack to cool for 10 minutes. Turn the cupcakes out of the pan to cool completely.

After filling the muffin cups half full with the chocolate cake batter, spoon on the remaining chocolate batter and all of the cream cheese batter to create a top that is half dark and half light.

Triple-Layer Chocolate Peanut Butter Cheesecake

CRUST

10 Fudge Cookies with White
  Chocolate (page 48)
1 cup unsalted peanuts
½ stick (¼ cup) unsalted butter, melted

CHOCOLATE LAYER

1½ pounds cream cheese
1½ cups (packed) light brown sugar
4 large eggs
1 cup sour cream
1 tablespoon vanilla extract
16 ounces semisweet chocolate, melted

PEANUT BUTTER LAYER

¾ cup creamy peanut butter
3 tablespoons unsalted butter
¾ cup powdered sugar
1 teaspoon vanilla extract

TOPPING

6 ounces milk chocolate, chopped
1 cup heavy cream
1 cup finely chopped unsalted peanuts

Yield: One 9-inch layered cheesecake

● Butter and flour the bottom of a 9-inch springform pan. Butter (but do not flour) a second 9-inch springform pan that is 3 inches deep.

● Make the crust: In a food processor, process the Fudge Cookies and peanuts to fine crumbs. Add the butter and process just until the crumbs are moistened. Press the crust mixture into the bottom and halfway up the sides of the 3-inch-deep springform.

● Preheat the oven to 300°F. Place a roasting pan partially filled with water below the rack the cheesecake will bake on.

● Prepare the chocolate layer: In a large bowl with an electric mixer, beat the cream cheese and sugar until smooth. Beat in the eggs one at a time, beating well after each addition. Beat in the sour cream and vanilla. Beat in the chocolate. Dividing the batter in half, pour into the prepared springform pans. Bake the cakes for 1 hour. Turn the oven off and leave the cheesecakes in the oven for 45 minutes. Cool in the pans on a rack for 30 minutes, then refrigerate until firm, about 4 hours. Remove the sides of the springforms.

● Make the peanut butter layer: In a medium bowl, blend the peanut butter and butter until smooth. Beat in the powdered sugar and vanilla. Spread the peanut butter mixture over the chilled cheesecake with the crust. Remove the cheesecake from the bottom of the other springform and invert on top of the peanut butter layer.

● Prepare the topping: Place the chocolate in a small bowl. In a small saucepan, bring the cream to a simmer. Pour over the chocolate. Let stand, covered, for 5 minutes, then stir until smooth. Refrigerate the ganache until chilled but not firm. With an electric mixer, slowly beat the ganache until thickened and smooth; be careful not to overbeat or the ganache will break.

● Spread the ganache on top of the cheesecake and halfway down the sides to meet the edge of the crust. Cover the ganache on the top and sides with the chopped peanuts.

Fudgy Studded Buttercream Cake

CAKE
1¾ cups all-purpose flour
1¾ cups granulated sugar
1 teaspoon baking soda
2 sticks (1 cup) unsalted butter
2 cups plus 2 tablespoons water
2½ cups unsweetened cocoa powder
2 large eggs
1 tablespoon vanilla extract
½ cup buttermilk

CHOCOLATE GANACHE
1 cup heavy cream
2 tablespoons granulated sugar

10 ounces semisweet chocolate,
 finely chopped

FUDGE FROSTING
2 sticks (1 cup) unsalted butter
½ cup unsweetened cocoa powder
2 teaspoons vanilla extract
4 cups powdered sugar
¼ cup milk
¾ cup chopped walnuts, toasted

Yield: One 9-inch layer cake

- Preheat the oven to 350°F. Butter and flour two 9-inch cake pans.

- Make the cake: In a small bowl, whisk together the flour, granulated sugar, and baking soda.

- In a heavy saucepan, combine the butter and water and cook until the butter is melted. Whisk in the cocoa and bring the mixture to a boil. Remove from the heat, transfer to a large bowl, and cool.

- Add the eggs, one at a time, to the cocoa mixture, beating well after each one. Beat in the vanilla. In two additions, alternately add the flour-sugar mixture and buttermilk, beating well after each addition.

- Pour the batter into the prepared pans and bake for 35 to 40 minutes, or until a cake tester inserted into the center comes out clean. Cool in the pans on a rack for 20 minutes. Then invert the cakes onto the racks to cool completely.

- Meanwhile, make the ganache: In a medium saucepan, bring the cream and granulated sugar to

a boil. Remove from the heat and stir in the chocolate until melted. Chill until firm enough to spread.

- Prepare the frosting: In a medium bowl with an electric mixer, cream the butter. Beat in the cocoa and vanilla. In three additions, alternately beat in the powdered sugar and milk. If the frosting is too soft to spread, chill.

- To assemble: Spread ¾ cup of ganache over the bottom layer. Top with the walnuts. Invert the top layer and spread ¾ cup of the fudge frosting on the bottom. Place the top layer, frosting-side down, on top of the bottom layer. Spread 1 cup of the frosting over the sides of the cake, and frost the top lightly with ½ cup. With a #21 star tip, pipe a ring of frosting rosettes around the outer rim of the cake. Then, with the same star tip, pipe a circle of ganache rosettes just inside the first ring. Continue alternating rings of frosting and ganache rosettes until the entire top of the cake is covered.

Coconut Almond Cake

CAKE

1½ cups all-purpose flour
½ teaspoon baking soda
¼ teaspoon salt
1 stick (½ cup) unsalted butter
1¼ cups granulated sugar
3 ounces almond paste (about ⅓ cup)
3 large eggs
1 teaspoon vanilla extract
¼ teaspoon almond extract
½ cup shredded coconut
½ cup milk

FUDGE FILLING

6 tablespoons unsalted butter
½ cup sweetened coconut cream

1½ ounces unsweetened chocolate,
  coarsely chopped
3½ ounces semisweet chocolate,
  coarsely chopped
1 ounce cream cheese, softened
¾ cup shredded coconut

TOPPING

1½ cups heavy cream
3 tablespoons powdered sugar
1½ teaspoons vanilla extract
¼ cup shredded coconut, toasted

Yield: One 9-inch layer cake

- Preheat the oven to 350°F. Butter a 9-inch cake pan. Line the bottom with a circle of wax paper, then butter and flour the paper.

- Make the cake: In a small bowl, whisk together the flour, baking soda, and salt.

- In a medium bowl with an electric mixer, cream the butter, granulated sugar, and almond paste. Beat in the eggs one at a time, beating well after each addition. Beat in the vanilla and almond extracts. Stir in the coconut.

- In three additions, alternately stir in the flour mixture and the milk, beating well after each addition.

- Pour the batter into the prepared pan. Bake for 45 to 50 minutes, or until a cake tester inserted in the center comes out clean. Set the cake pan on a wire rack to cool for 20 minutes. Then invert the cake onto the rack to cool completely.

- Meanwhile, make the fudge filling: In a small saucepan, melt the butter with the coconut cream. Remove from the heat and stir in the unsweetened chocolate and 1½ ounces of the semisweet chocolate. Stir until melted and smooth.

- Beat in the cream cheese and coconut. Let cool slightly, then stir in the remaining 2 ounces chopped semisweet chocolate. Cool the filling until firm but still spreadable.

- To assemble: With a serrated knife, cut the cake horizontally into two layers. Place one layer cut side up and spread with the cooled fudge filling. Top with the second layer.

- Make the topping: In a large bowl, beat the cream with the powdered sugar and vanilla until soft peaks form. Spread the whipped cream over the cake and sprinkle with the toasted coconut. Serve immediately.

Ganache-Filled Devil's Food Cake

CAKE
1¾ cups boiling water
6 ounces semisweet chocolate,
 coarsely chopped
1 cup unsweetened cocoa powder
2 cups sifted cake flour
2 teaspoons baking soda
¼ teaspoon salt
10 ounces unsalted butter, softened
1¾ cups (packed) dark brown sugar
4 large eggs
2 teaspoons vanilla extract

CHOCOLATE GANACHE
½ cup heavy cream
2 tablespoons unsalted butter
4 ounces semisweet chocolate, finely chopped

CHOCOLATE FROSTING
2½ sticks (1¼ cups) plus 2 tablespoons
 unsalted butter, softened
4½ cups powdered sugar
1 cup unsweetened cocoa powder
2 teaspoons vanilla extract
¼ cup plus 2 tablespoons milk

Yield: One 9-inch layer cake

- Make the cake: Preheat the oven to 350°F. Butter two 9-inch cake pans. Line the bottoms with circles of wax paper, then butter and flour the paper.

- In a medium bowl, pour the boiling water over the chopped chocolate. Set aside for 5 minutes. Add the cocoa and stir until the mixture is smooth. Set aside to cool to room temperature.

- In a small bowl, whisk together the flour, baking soda, and salt.

- In a large bowl with an electric mixer, cream the butter and brown sugar. Add the eggs one at a time, beating well after each addition. Beat in the vanilla. Add the flour mixture and half of the chocolate mixture. Beat on low speed to combine, then on high for 1½ minutes. Add the remaining chocolate mixture and beat the batter on low speed to combine.

- Pour the batter into the prepared pans and bake for 30 to 40 minutes, or until a cake tester inserted in the center comes out clean. Set the cake pans on a wire rack to cool for 20 minutes. Then invert the cakes onto the racks to cool completely.

- Prepare the ganache: In a small saucepan, bring the cream and butter to a simmer. Add the chocolate, cover for 5 minutes, then stir until smooth. Refrigerate the ganache until firm enough to spread.

- Meanwhile, make the frosting: In a large bowl with an electric mixer, cream the butter. In a medium bowl, whisk together the sugar and cocoa. Beat one-third of the sugar-cocoa mixture into the butter. Mix in the vanilla. Add the rest of the sugar-cocoa mixture alternately with the milk and beat until the frosting is smooth.

- Assemble the cake: Top one cake layer with the ganache. Add the second layer of cake and frost the sides of the cake, then the top. Decoratively pipe frosting around the base and top edges of the cake.

167

Skinny Fallen Mousse Cake with Berry Sauce

CAKE
¼ cup whole almonds, toasted
¾ cup granulated sugar
½ cup unsweetened cocoa powder, sifted
5 tablespoons boiling water
2 ounces sweet chocolate, finely chopped
1 teaspoon vanilla extract
2 large eggs, separated, plus 2 egg whites
3 tablespoons all-purpose flour
¼ teaspoon cream of tartar

BERRY SAUCE
3 cups whole strawberries
2 cups raspberries
Powdered sugar, for dusting

Yield: 12 servings

- Make the cake: Preheat the oven to 375°F. Line the bottom of an 8½-inch springform pan with a circle of wax paper. Lightly spray the wax paper and sides of the pan with nonstick cooking spray.

- In a food processor, grind the toasted almonds for 2 to 3 seconds, or just until ground; do not over-process or the nuts will be oily.

- In a double boiler, blend ½ cup of the sugar with the cocoa and 2 tablespoons of the boiling water. Add the 3 remaining tablespoons boiling water and stir until smooth. Add the sweet chocolate and stir over hot, not simmering, water, until the chocolate is melted. Stir in the vanilla, remove from the heat, and set aside.

- In a small bowl, beat the egg yolks until thick and pale. Whisk about ¼ cup of the chocolate mixture into the eggs to warm them. Transfer the warmed eggs to the chocolate mixture and stir to combine. Stir in the flour and ground almonds and set aside.

- In a large bowl, beat the 4 egg whites until foamy. Add the cream of tartar and beat until soft peaks form. Add the remaining ¼ cup sugar and beat until stiff peaks form.

- Stir one-fourth of the egg whites into the chocolate mixture to lighten it, then gently but thoroughly fold in the remaining egg whites. Spread the batter in the prepared pan and bake for 25 minutes, or until a cake tester inserted in the center comes out clean. Set the pan on a wire rack to cool completely.

- Make the sauce: In a food processor, purée 2 cups of the strawberries and 1 cup of the raspberries. Strain through a fine-mesh sieve to remove the seeds. Slice the remaining 1 cup strawberries and stir the sliced strawberries and remaining raspberries into the strained purée.

- To serve, remove the sides of the pan. Dust with powdered sugar, cut into 12 wedges, and serve the berry sauce on the side.

"Light" Chocolate Cheesecake

CRUST
1 cup chocolate wafer cookie crumbs
2 tablespoons granulated sugar
1 tablespoon water

FILLING
1 cup (packed) dark brown sugar
¼ cup unsweetened cocoa powder
¼ cup all-purpose flour

16 ounces nonfat cream cheese
1 cup light sour cream
4 large egg whites
1½ ounces German sweet chocolate, melted and cooled
2 teaspoons vanilla extract

Yield: 10 servings

- Preheat the oven to 300°F. Spray the sides and bottom of an 8½-inch springform pan with nonstick cooking spray. Place a shallow roasting pan of water on the bottom rack of the oven.

- Prepare the crust: In a medium bowl, use your fingers or a fork to toss the cookie crumbs with the granulated sugar and water until evenly moistened. Press the crumb mixture into the bottom and one-third of the way up the sides of the springform pan.

- Make the filling: In a small bowl, blend the brown sugar, cocoa, and flour. In a food processor, process the cream cheese and flour-cocoa mixture until smooth. Add the sour cream and blend until smooth. Add the egg whites and blend. Add the melted chocolate and vanilla and blend.

- Pour the filling into the crust and place the cheesecake on the center rack of the oven. Bake for 1 hour, or until the filling is just set (it will still be wobbly in the center). Turn off the heat but leave the cake in the oven for another 30 minutes. Remove from the oven and cool in the pan on a wire rack. Cover and refrigerate until well chilled, at least 8 hours or overnight.

- To serve, run a knife around the edges of the cake to loosen it from the side of the springform, then remove the sides of the pan.

Raspberry and White Chocolate Tart

CHOCOLATE TART SHELL
1 cup all-purpose flour
¼ cup unsweetened cocoa powder
4 tablespoons granulated sugar
¼ teaspoon salt
6 tablespoons cold unsalted butter, cut
  into small pieces
1 large egg yolk
1 teaspoon vanilla extract
2 to 3 tablespoons ice water

WHITE CHOCOLATE CUSTARD
1 cup heavy cream
2 egg yolks
1 tablespoon granulated sugar
1 tablespoon cornstarch
6 ounces white chocolate, finely chopped
1 pint fresh raspberries
Powdered sugar, for dusting

Yield: One 9-inch tart

● Make the tart shell: In a food processor, combine the flour, cocoa, sugar, and salt and process briefly. Add the butter and pulse until the mixture resembles coarse meal. In a small bowl, lightly beat the egg yolk with the vanilla. With the machine running, drizzle in the egg yolk mixture through the feed tube, then drizzle enough of the water so that the dough begins to gather into a ball. Scrape the dough from the work bowl, flatten into a disk, and wrap with plastic wrap. Chill for 1 hour.

● Prepare the white chocolate custard: In a small heavy saucepan, stir together the sugar and cornstarch. Gradually whisk in the cream. Bring to a boil over medium-low heat, stirring constantly. In a small bowl, beat the egg yolks. Gradually whisk the cream into the yolks and return the mixture to the saucepan. Cook over low heat, stirring constantly, until the custard is very thick and steamy; do not allow it to boil. Remove from the heat and stir in the white chocolate. Transfer to a bowl, place a sheet of plastic wrap directly on the surface of the custard, and refrigerate until well chilled, about 2 hours.

● Remove the dough from the refrigerator and let stand for 10 minutes. On a lightly floured surface, roll the dough out to an 11-inch round. Transfer to a 9-inch tart pan with a removable bottom and press dough into the bottom and sides. Freeze the tart shell for 15 minutes.

● Meanwhile, preheat the oven to 400°F. Bake the tart shell for 18 minutes, or until set. Cool on a wire rack.

● Assemble the tart: Spread the white chocolate custard evenly into the tart shell. Arrange the raspberries over the surface of the tart and dust with powdered sugar.

Chocolate Pecan Tartlets

PASTRY

2 cups all-purpose flour
2 sticks (1 cup) salted butter
2 large egg yolks
2 to 3 tablespoons ice water

FILLING

1 stick (½ cup) salted butter
4 ounces unsweetened baking
  chocolate
2 large eggs
1 cup (packed) dark brown sugar

½ cup corn syrup
2 teaspoons vanilla extract
1½ cups pecans, chopped

TOPPING

24 pecan halves
½ cup heavy cream
¼ cup granulated sugar
1 teaspoon vanilla extract

Yield: Twenty-four 2½-inch tartlets

- Prepare pastry: In medium bowl, combine flour and butter with pastry cutter until dough resembles coarse meal. Add egg yolks and water, then mix with a fork just until dough can be shaped into a ball.

- Gather dough into a ball. Wrap tightly in plastic wrap or a plastic bag. Refrigerate until firm—about 1 hour.

- Prepare filling: In a 2-quart saucepan combine butter and chocolate, stirring constantly over low heat. Transfer to medium bowl and let cool for 5 minutes. With an electric mixer on medium speed, beat eggs into chocolate mixture. Add sugar, corn syrup, and vanilla, and blend on low speed until smooth. Fold in pecans.

- Preheat oven to 350°F.

- Assemble tartlets: On lightly floured counter or board, use a lightly floured rolling pin to roll out dough to ⅛-inch thickness. Using a 2½-inch fluted tartlet pan as a guide, cut dough ¼ inch around entire edge. Repeat with remaining dough. Lay dough rounds in tartlet pans and press in firmly.

- Fill pans ⅔ full of chocolate pecan filling. Place on baking sheet to catch any drips. Bake for 30 to 35 minutes, or until filling is set and does not look wet.

- While still warm, place a pecan half in center of each tartlet. Meanwhile, chill mixing bowl and beaters in freezer.

- Prepare topping: In a medium bowl with electric mixer set on high, beat cream, sugar, and vanilla until stiff peaks form. Do not overbeat. Transfer the whipped topping to a pastry bag fitted with a medium star tip, and pipe decorative topping onto each tartlet.

171

Caramel Chocolate Tartlets

PASTRY
1½ cups all-purpose flour
¼ cup granulated sugar
1 stick (½ cup) salted butter, chilled
2 large egg yolks
1 teaspoon vanilla extract
4 to 5 tablespoons ice water

CARAMEL FILLING
1½ sticks (¾ cup) salted butter
1 cup (packed) dark brown sugar
⅓ cup light corn syrup
3 tablespoons heavy cream
One 16-ounce solid semisweet or milk
* chocolate bar, at room temperature*

Yield: 8 tartlets

- Prepare pastry: In a medium bowl, combine flour, sugar, and butter with a pastry cutter until dough resembles coarse meal. Add egg yolks and vanilla. Gradually add ice water until dough can be shaped into a ball. Or, use a food processor fitted with a metal blade to combine flour, sugar, and butter until dough resembles coarse meal. Add egg yolks, vanilla, and ice water by tablespoons, and process until dough begins to form a ball.

- Flatten dough into a disk and wrap tightly in plastic wrap or place in plastic bag. Chill 1 hour or until firm.

- On floured board using a floured rolling pin, roll out dough to ¼ inch thickness. Cut 4-inch rounds to fit into 3½-inch-diameter tart pans. Gently press into tart pans and place in refrigerator for 15 minutes. Preheat oven to 400°F.

- Remove tart shells from refrigerator and prick bottom with a fork. Bake 13 to 15 minutes or until edges begin to turn golden brown. Cool tart shells to room temperature.

- Prepare the caramel filling: Combine butter, brown sugar, and corn syrup in a heavy 2-quart saucepan. Place over medium heat, and stir constantly until sugar dissolves. Turn heat to high and boil without stirring for 2 minutes, or until large bubbles form.

- Remove from heat and stir in cream. Cool caramel 5 minutes and then pour into tart shells. Cool caramel tartlets to room temperature. Use a vegetable peeler to slowly and carefully shave curls from the chocolate bar. Sprinkle tartlets with chocolate curls.

As you press the 4-inch rounds into the tart pans, press the excess dough off the top edge (left). Chill the lined pans for 15 minutes, then use a fork to prick holes in the bottom of each crust (left, below)—this will keep the bottom from ballooning up during baking.

Lemon Custard Cake

CAKE

1½ cups cake flour
1 cup granulated sugar
¾ teaspoon baking powder
½ teaspoon salt
1½ sticks (¾ cup) unsalted butter, softened
¼ cup sour cream
2 large eggs, at room temperature
¼ cup lemon juice
2 teaspoons grated lemon zest
½ teaspoon lemon extract

VANILLA CUSTARD

1 cup heavy cream
1 large egg
2 large egg yolks
⅓ cup granulated sugar
1 tablespoon plus 2 teaspoons cornstarch
1 teaspoon vanilla extract

CHOCOLATE GANACHE

6 ounces semisweet chocolate, finely chopped
¾ cup heavy cream
2 tablespoons unsalted butter
2 tablespoons granulated sugar

Yield: One 9-inch layer cake

- Preheat the oven to 350°F. Grease a 9-inch cake pan, line the bottom with a circle of wax paper, then grease and flour the paper.

- Make the cake: In a large bowl, mix the flour, sugar, baking powder, and salt. Add the butter, sour cream, and 1 egg. Mix until just blended. Add the remaining egg, the lemon juice, zest, and extract. Beat until smooth.

- Scrape batter into pan and bake for 40 to 45 minutes, or until top is golden and a cake tester inserted in the center comes out clean. Set the cake pan on a wire rack to cool for 20 minutes. Then invert cake onto rack to cool completely. Wrap cake in plastic wrap and chill in freezer until slightly firm, about 15 minutes.

- Meanwhile, make the custard: In a small saucepan, bring cream to a simmer. In a bowl, beat whole egg, egg yolks, sugar, and cornstarch together until light and lemon-colored, about 3 minutes. Gradually whisk hot cream into egg mixture to warm it. Transfer warmed egg mixture to saucepan and cook over medium heat, stirring constantly, until thick, about 2 minutes. Remove from heat and stir in vanilla. Strain the custard through a fine sieve and set in a large bowl of ice water to quick-cool to room temperature. Cover and refrigerate until thoroughly chilled.

- Prepare the ganache: Place the chocolate in a medium bowl. In a small saucepan, bring the cream and butter to a simmer. Stir in the sugar. Pour the hot cream mixture over the chocolate. Let stand, covered, for 5 minutes, then stir until smooth. Let cool to room temperature.

- Assemble: With a long serrated knife, slice chilled cake horizontally into two layers. Place bottom cake layer on a 9-inch cardboard round. Place layer on a rack set over a cookie sheet. Spread top of cake with the chilled vanilla custard. Gently top with the second cake layer. Spread the ganache evenly over sides and top of cake. Refrigerate for 20 minutes to set.

Chocolate Raspberry Rhapsody

CHOCOLATE RING
1¼ cups semisweet chocolate chips
1 cup granulated sugar
½ cup boiling water
2 sticks (1 cup) unsalted butter, softened
4 large eggs
2 tablespoons raspberry liqueur
2 teaspoons vanilla extract
⅛ teaspoon salt

RASPBERRY CREAM
1 cup heavy cream
2 tablespoons seedless red raspberry jam
2 tablespoons granulated sugar
2 teaspoons vanilla extract
Fresh raspberries, for garnish

Yield: 16 servings

- Preheat the oven to 350°F. Spray a 5-cup ring mold with nonstick cooking spray.

- Make the chocolate ring: In a food processor, combine the chocolate chips and sugar, then process until finely chopped. Add the boiling water and process until melted and smooth. Add the butter in three additions, processing briefly each time. Add the eggs, liqueur, vanilla, and salt. Process until well blended.

- Pour the mixture into the prepared ring mold. Place the mold in a larger pan and fill the pan with 2 inches of boiling water. Bake for 1 hour, or until firm to the touch; a knife inserted into the center should come out clean.

- Remove the mold from the water bath and let cool for 1 hour on a rack. Cover and refrigerate for at least 3 hours.

- Make the raspberry cream: In a small bowl, beat the cream with the jam, sugar, and vanilla until soft peaks form.

- Assemble: Run a knife around the edges of the mold and invert the ring onto a serving dish. Pipe a ring of raspberry cream rosettes around the base of the ring. Fill the center of the ring with the remaining raspberry cream. Garnish the ring with fresh raspberries.

Double-Fudge Chip Cake

CAKE

3 ounces unsweetened chocolate,
  finely chopped
2¼ cups sifted cake flour
2 teaspoons baking soda
½ teaspoon salt
1 stick (½ cup) salted butter, softened
2¼ cups (packed) light brown sugar
3 large eggs, at room temperature
1½ teaspoons vanilla extract
1 cup sour cream
1 cup boiling water

FROSTING

8 ounces unsweetened chocolate,
  finely chopped
2 sticks (1 cup) unsalted butter, softened
2 pounds powdered sugar
1 cup heavy cream
4 teaspoons vanilla extract
6 ounces milk chocolate chips (1 cup)
1 package chocolate kisses, for garnish

Yield: One 9-inch layer cake

- Preheat the oven to 350°F. Grease and flour three 9-inch cake pans.

- Make the cake: In a double boiler, melt the chocolate over hot, not simmering, water. Set aside to cool.

- In a medium bowl, combine the flour, baking soda, and salt.

- In a large bowl with an electric mixer, cream the butter. Add the brown sugar and then the eggs, one at a time, blending well after each addition. Beat at high speed for 5 minutes. Beat in the vanilla and the melted chocolate.

- Beat in portions of the flour mixture alternately with the sour cream, beginning and ending with the flour mixture; beat well after each addition.

- Stir in the boiling water and pour the batter at once into the prepared pans. Bake for 35 minutes, or until the center springs back when touched lightly. Set the cake pans on a rack to cool for 10 minutes.

Then invert the cakes onto the racks to cool completely.

- Prepare the frosting: In a double boiler, melt the chocolate with the butter. Set aside to cool to room temperature.

- In a medium bowl with an electric mixer, blend the powdered sugar, cream, and vanilla until smooth. Add the cooled chocolate mixture and mix at low speed until blended. Place the frosting in the refrigerator until thick and firm yet still easy to spread, 20 to 30 minutes.

- Assemble: Place one cake layer upside down on a cake dish. Spread one-fourth of frosting on top and sprinkle with ½ cup of the chips. Add a second cake layer upside down and frost with another one-fourth of the frosting and the remaining ½ cup chips. Add the top layer upside down and frost the top and sides of the cake with the remaining frosting. Garnish the cake with the chocolate kisses.

175

Chocolate Cream Roll

CAKE
6 ounces semisweet chocolate,
  coarsely chopped
6 large eggs, separated
¼ cup granulated sugar
1 teaspoon vanilla extract
½ teaspoon cream of tartar

CREAM FILLING
1 cup heavy cream
2 tablespoons powdered sugar
1 teaspoon vanilla extract
2 teaspoons unsweetened cocoa powder
Fudge Sauce (page 211)

Yield: 12 servings

- Preheat the oven to 350°F. Line a 12-by-17-inch jelly-roll pan with foil. Grease and flour the foil.

- Make the cake: In a double boiler, melt the chocolate over hot, not simmering, water. Set aside to cool slightly.

- In a medium bowl with an electric mixer, beat the egg yolks and granulated sugar until light and lemon-colored, about 5 minutes. Blend in the chocolate and vanilla. Set aside.

- In another medium bowl, beat the egg whites until soft peaks form. Add the cream of tartar and beat until stiff peaks form. Stir one-fourth of the beaten whites into the chocolate mixture to lighten it. Gently but thoroughly fold in the remaining whites. Immediately transfer the batter to the prepared pan and smooth the top of the batter.

- Bake for 15 minutes, or until the center of the cake springs back when lightly pressed. Cover the cake with a damp kitchen towel and cool to room temperature on a rack.

- Prepare the filling: In a medium bowl, whip the cream with the powdered sugar and vanilla until stiff peaks form.

- Assemble: Very gently lift the cake out of the pan along with the foil. Dust the top of the cake evenly with the cocoa. Spread the surface with the whipped cream, leaving a 1-inch border along the cake edges. With a long end toward you, roll up the cake, gently removing the foil as you go.

- To serve, drizzle some of the Fudge Sauce onto a plate and place a slice of the cake roll on top of the sauce. Serve any remaining sauce at the table.

Chocolate Shortbread

CHOCOLATE SHORTBREAD

1½ sticks (¾ cup) unsalted butter, softened
¾ cup powdered sugar, sifted
2 teaspoons vanilla extract
1 cup plus 2 tablespoons all-purpose flour
½ cup unsweetened cocoa powder
2 ounces semisweet chocolate, finely grated

WHITE AND DARK GANACHES

6 ounces white chocolate, coarsely chopped
6 ounces semisweet chocolate,
  coarsely chopped
1 tablespoon granulated sugar
⅔ cup heavy cream
2 tablespoons unsalted butter

Yield: 8 servings

- Bake the shortbread: Preheat the oven to 350°F. Generously grease a 9-inch glass pie plate.

- In a large bowl, beat the butter until creamy. Beat in the powdered sugar until well combined. Beat in the vanilla.

- In a small bowl, combine the flour and cocoa. Add the flour-cocoa mixture and the grated chocolate to the dough and beat in just until combined. The mixture will be crumbly.

- Using your hands, shape the dough into a large disk. Place the disk in the prepared pie plate and press it evenly over the bottom of the plate (do not go up the sides). With a fork, prick the dough all the way through, at ½-inch intervals.

- Bake for 25 to 30 minutes, or until just set. Cool in the pie plate on a rack for 10 minutes. While the shortbread is still warm, cut into 8 wedges with a thin, sharp knife. Let the wedges cool completely in the pan.

- Make the ganaches: Place the white chocolate and semisweet chocolate in two separate medium bowls; add the sugar to the semisweet chocolate. In a small saucepan, bring the cream and butter to a simmer. Pour ⅓ cup of the hot cream over the white chocolate. Pour the remaining ⅓ cup cream over the semisweet chocolate. Let both stand, covered, for 5 minutes; stir until smooth. Let cool to room temperature, then refrigerate until slightly firm, about 20 minutes. Whisk the ganaches to a consistency thick enough to be piped through a pastry bag.

- Place the white and dark ganaches in pastry bags fitted with a #21 star tip. Pipe alternating rows of white and dark ganache rosettes, starting with white ganache at the wider end of the shortbread.

Fudge-Glazed Chocolate Hazelnut Torte

CAKE

1½ cups hazelnuts, roasted and skinned
4 ounces semisweet chocolate,
  coarsely chopped
⅓ cup plain, unseasoned dried bread crumbs
1 stick (½ cup) unsalted butter
1¼ cups granulated sugar
6 large eggs, separated
1 teaspoon vanilla extract
½ teaspoon cream of tartar

GANACHE

6 ounces semisweet chocolate, finely chopped
¾ cup heavy cream
1 tablespoon unsalted butter
1 tablespoon granulated sugar

Whipped cream rosettes, for garnish

Yield: 10 to 12 servings

- Preheat the oven to 350°F. Grease and flour the bottom and sides of a 9½-inch springform pan; line the bottom with parchment or wax paper and butter the paper.

- Make the cake: In a food processor, process the hazelnuts with the chocolate until finely ground and just beginning to form a paste, about 30 seconds. In a medium bowl, combine the chocolate-hazelnut mixture and bread crumbs.

- In a large bowl, cream the butter with 1 cup of the sugar. Beat in the egg yolks and vanilla. Beat in the chocolate-hazelnut mixture just until blended.

- In a medium bowl, beat the egg whites until foamy. Beat in the cream of tartar, then gradually add the remaining ¼ cup sugar and beat until stiff but not dry peaks form. Stir one-fourth of the egg whites into the batter to lighten it. Gently but thoroughly fold in the remaining egg whites.

- Scrape the batter into the prepared pan. Bake for

45 to 50 minutes, or until a cake tester inserted into the center comes out clean.

- Set on a wire rack to cool for 40 minutes. Loosen the cake with a knife and remove the sides of the pan; let the cake cool completely. Remove the cake from the pan bottom, remove the paper, and set the cake right-side up on a rack. Place the rack over a baking sheet.

- Make the ganache: Place the chocolate in a medium bowl. In a small saucepan, bring the cream and butter to a simmer. Stir in the sugar. Pour the hot cream mixture over the chocolate. Let stand, covered, for 5 minutes, then stir until smooth. Let cool to lukewarm.

- Pour the ganache over the cake allowing it to run down the sides. Smooth the top surface. Place in the refrigerator for about 15 minutes to set the ganache. Serve garnished with rosettes of whipped cream.

Mrs. Fields' Macadamia Nut Tart

PASTRY CRUST
1¾ cups all-purpose flour
¼ cup granulated sugar
1 stick (½ cup) salted butter, chilled
2 large egg yolks
3 tablespoons ice water

FILLING
1 cup corn syrup
1 stick (½ cup) plus 3 tablespoons salted butter

1 cup granulated sugar
2 tablespoons unsulfurized molasses
¼ teaspoon salt
2 large eggs, lightly beaten
1 teaspoon vanilla extract
2½ cups unsalted dry-roasted
  macadamia nuts
Whipped cream (optional)

Yield: 12 servings

- Prepare the crust: Combine flour, sugar, and butter, and work with a pastry cutter until dough resembles coarse meal. Add egg yolks and water, and mix with a fork just until dough can be shaped into a ball. Or, using a food processor fitted with a metal blade, combine flour, sugar, and butter. Process until dough resembles coarse meal. Add egg yolks and water and process just until a ball begins to form.

- Shape dough into a disk and wrap tightly in plastic wrap or plastic bag. Chill in refrigerator 1 hour or until firm.

- Prepare the filling: Combine the corn syrup, butter, sugar, molasses, and salt in a double boiler. Bring to a boil over medium heat, stirring occasionally. Remove from heat and cool to room temperature. Once cool, add the eggs and vanilla and stir until smooth. Set syrup mixture aside until ready to use. (Mixture can be made up to 2 days in advance and refrigerated until it is ready to use.)

- Assemble the tart: Preheat oven to 300°F. Spray nonstick cooking spray on an 8- or 9-inch tart pan with a removable bottom.

- On a floured board using a floured rolling pin, roll out dough to a 10-inch circle, ¼ inch thick. Place pastry in pan, lightly pressing it into the bottom and sides. Roll off excess dough from the top edge with rolling pin.

- Fill the pastry shell with the macadamia nuts. Pour filling over nuts and bake 90 minutes or until golden brown. Let pie cool, remove sides of pan and garnish with whipped cream, if desired.

Fold the dough in half, then drape it over the prepared tart pan (right, top). Gently press the dough into the pan. Be sure that there is enough dough pressed into the fluted edges to support the filling when baked. Use a rolling pin to roll off the excess dough (right, bottom).

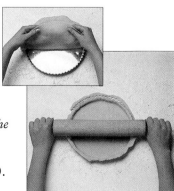

Debbi's Deadly Chocolate Muffins

12 ounces semisweet chocolate,
   coarsely chopped
1 stick (½ cup) unsalted butter
½ cup sour cream
1 cup sifted cake flour
½ teaspoon baking soda
¼ teaspoon salt
4 large eggs

½ cup (packed) light brown sugar
1 teaspoon vanilla extract
1¼ cups semisweet chocolate chips
¼ cup coarsely chopped macadamia nuts
¼ cup white chocolate chips

Yield: 12 muffins

- Preheat the oven to 350°F. Lightly oil the top surface of a 12-cup muffin tin. Line the cups with paper liners.

- In a double boiler, melt the chopped semisweet chocolate with the butter and stir until smooth. Remove from the heat and stir in the sour cream.

- In a small bowl, whisk together the flour, baking soda, and salt.

- In a large bowl with an electric mixer, beat the eggs and sugar until light and pale, about 5 minutes. Beat in the chocolate mixture and the vanilla. Add the flour mixture and 1 cup of the semisweet chocolate chips.

- Spoon the batter evenly into the prepared muffin cups. Top with the remaining ¼ cup semisweet chips, the macadamia nuts, and the white chocolate chips. Bake for 20 to 25 minutes, or until the centers are set.

- Set the muffin tin on a wire rack to cool for 15 minutes. Then remove the muffins to cool completely.

Banana Nut Bread

2½ cups all-purpose flour
1½ teaspoons baking soda
½ teaspoon salt
1½ sticks (¾ cup) salted butter, softened
1½ cups (packed) light brown sugar
2 large eggs

3 cups ripe bananas (about 7 medium), mashed
1 teaspoon vanilla extract
1 cup (4 ounces) chopped walnuts

Yield: Thirty ½-inch slices (15 slices per loaf)

- Preheat oven to 325°F. Grease two 9-by-5-inch loaf pans.

- In a medium bowl combine flour, soda and salt with a wire whisk; set aside.

- In a large bowl cream butter and sugar with an electric mixer. Add eggs, bananas and vanilla, and beat at medium speed until thick. Scrape down sides of bowl.

- Add the flour mixture and walnuts, then blend at low speed just until combined. Do not overmix.

- Pour batter into prepared pans. Bake on center rack of oven for 60 to 70 minutes. A toothpick inserted in center should come out clean, and the bread should pull away from the sides.

- Cool in pan, for 10 minutes. Turn pans on sides; cool to room temperature before removing and slicing.

181

Chocolate Chip Banana Bread

3 cups all-purpose flour
2 teaspoons baking powder
1 teaspoon salt
1½ sticks (¾ cup) unsalted butter, softened
2 cups granulated sugar
3 cups mashed bananas (about 8)

4 large eggs, well beaten
2 teaspoons vanilla extract
1 cup mini semisweet chocolate chips

Yield: Two 9-inch loaves

- Preheat the oven to 350°F. Lightly butter two 9-by-5-inch loaf pans. Line the bottoms with buttered parchment or wax paper.

- In a bowl, whisk together the flour, baking powder, and salt.

- In a medium bowl, cream the butter and sugar. Add the bananas and eggs, beating until well blended. Beat in the vanilla.

- Add the dry ingredients to the banana mixture and blend well. Stir in the semisweet chocolate chips. Do not overmix.

- Pour the batter into the prepared pans and bake for 55 to 60 minutes, or until golden brown and a cake tester inserted in the center comes out clean. Set the pans on a rack to cool for 15 minutes. Then turn out of the pans to cool completely.

Puddings, Soufflés, and Frozen Desserts

Bread Pudding

12 slices raisin nut bread
1 stick (½ cup) salted butter, at room temperature
2 butter croissants, sliced lengthwise into
 ¼-inch slices
6 large eggs
1 cup plus ⅛ teaspoon granulated sugar, divided

1 tablespoon vanilla extract
4 cups (1 quart) light cream or half-and-half
½ teaspoon ground cinnamon
⅛ teaspoon ground nutmeg

Yield: 12 servings

- Preheat oven to 325°F. Butter sides and bottom of 9-by-13-inch baking pan.

- Butter one side of each bread slice and layer in pan alternately with croissants (6 slices bread, croissant slices, 6 slices bread).

- In a large bowl with an electric mixer set on medium-high speed beat eggs until slightly thickened, about 5 minutes. Add sugar and vanilla and beat at medium speed until thoroughly combined. Reduce speed to low and add cream; mix until smooth.

- Pour egg-cream mixture over bread and croissant slices. The slices will absorb egg-cream mixture

slowly, so continue adding liquid until all is in pan.

- In a small bowl combine cinnamon, nutmeg and ⅛ teaspoon sugar. Sprinkle sugar-spice mixture over the bread pudding.

- Fill a baking pan larger than the 9-by-13-inch bread pudding pan halfway up with hot water. Place in oven. Set bread pudding pan in the water bath. Bake for 45 to 50 minutes or until custard is set. When set, remove bread pudding from the oven, and discard water in larger pan. Cool to room temperature. Refrigerate for 2 hours or until firm.

Homestyle Chocolate Pudding

1 cup granulated sugar
¼ cup cornstarch
¼ cup plus 2 tablespoons unsweetened
   cocoa powder
⅛ teaspoon salt

4 cups heavy cream
2 large egg yolks, lightly beaten
2 teaspoons vanilla extract

Yield: 4 to 6 servings

- In a heavy medium saucepan, stir together the sugar, cornstarch, cocoa powder, and salt. Gradually whisk in the cream and egg yolks.

- Place over medium heat and cook, stirring frequently, until the mixture comes to a boil, about 20 minutes. Simmer, stirring constantly, for 1 minute, then remove from the heat and stir in the vanilla.

- Transfer the pudding to a serving bowl, cover, and refrigerate until well chilled.

- Note: For a light version of the pudding, use low-fat (1%) milk in place of the heavy cream and increase the cornstarch to ¼ cup plus 1 tablespoon.

185

Chocolate Caramel Custard

CARAMEL
1½ cups granulated sugar
¼ cup water

CHOCOLATE CUSTARD
8 egg yolks
½ cup granulated sugar
2 cups light cream

6 ounces semisweet chocolate, finely chopped
1 teaspoon vanilla extract

Whipped cream and chocolate shavings,
 for garnish

Yield: 8 servings

- Preheat the oven to 325°F.

- Make the caramel: In a small heavy saucepan, dissolve the sugar in the water over low heat. Bring to a boil over medium-high heat, stirring constantly, then let boil without stirring until the syrup turns a deep amber. Quickly remove from the heat and pour an equal quantity of caramel syrup into each of eight 4-ounce ramekins. Place the ramekins in a large baking dish or roasting pan. Set aside.

- Prepare the chocolate custard: In a medium bowl, combine the egg yolks and sugar until smooth.

- In a medium saucepan, bring the cream to a simmer. Gradually whisk the hot cream into the yolk-sugar mixture. Add the chocolate and vanilla and stir until smooth.

- Strain the custard mixture through a sieve. Dividing evenly, pour the custard into the prepared ramekins. Pour hot water into the baking dish (or roasting pan) to come halfway up the sides of the ramekins. Bake the custards in the middle of the oven for about 30 minutes, or until they are set. Remove from hot water and set on wire racks to cool to room temperature.

- Cover and refrigerate for at least 4 hours or overnight. Serve with a rosette of whipped cream and chocolate shavings.

White Chocolate Cream with Apricots

¼ cup diced dried apricots
¼ cup apricot brandy
5 large egg yolks
¼ cup granulated sugar
2 cups heavy cream
5 ounces white chocolate, finely chopped

½ teaspoon vanilla extract
2 ounces semisweet chocolate, finely chopped
½ teaspoon vegetable oil

Yield: 6 servings

- Preheat the oven to 325°F.

- In a small bowl, combine the apricots and apricot brandy and set aside.

- In a medium bowl, whisk the egg yolks and sugar. In a medium saucepan, bring the cream to a simmer over medium heat. Remove the pan from the heat. Add the white chocolate and stir until melted and smooth, about 5 minutes. Slowly whisk the warm white chocolate mixture into the egg yolks. Whisk in the vanilla.

- Measure out 2 teaspoons of the brandy that the apricots are soaking in and stir it into the custard. Set aside the remaining apricots until serving time.

- Arrange six 4-ounce ramekins or custard cups in a roasting pan. Spoon the custard into the cups. Fill the pan with enough hot water to come halfway up the sides of the cups. Bake for 35 minutes, or until the custard is set. Remove the custards from the water and cool on wire racks. Refrigerate until thoroughly chilled, about 4 hours.

- In a double boiler, melt the semisweet chocolate with the oil over hot, not simmering, water. Set aside to cool slightly. Drain the apricots and discard the brandy.

- Spoon the warm chocolate into a pastry bag fitted with a very small round tip. Top the chilled custards with the drained, diced apricots and pipe the apricots with the chocolate.

187

Double-Chocolate Trifle

2 cups heavy cream
10 ounces semisweet chocolate, finely chopped
3 tablespoons granulated sugar
Pinch of salt
4 large egg yolks
1 teaspoon vanilla extract
1 pound of chocolate pound cake, cut into
¼-inch-thick slices

⅓ cup coffee liqueur
1 pint strawberries, cut into thin slices
Whipped cream and unsweetened cocoa
powder, for garnish

Yield: 8 to 10 servings

- In a double boiler, heat the cream with the chocolate, sugar, and salt, stirring frequently, until the mixture is melted and smooth.

- In a medium bowl, lightly beat the egg yolks. Whisk about one-fourth of the chocolate cream into the yolks to warm them. Transfer the warmed yolks to the chocolate cream in the double boiler and cook over simmering water, stirring frequently, until the custard just begins to thicken.

- Pour the custard into a large bowl and stir in the vanilla. Place a piece of plastic wrap directly on the filling to prevent a skin from forming and set aside.

- Stack the cake slices and cut them into quarters (there should be about 5 cups). Place half of the cake slices in the bottom of a 2-quart, straight-sided, flat-bottomed bowl (preferably glass). Sprinkle the cake with half of the coffee liqueur. Top with half of the chocolate custard and half of the sliced strawberries. Repeat the layering.

- Cover and chill for 2 to 3 hours. Just before serving, pipe rosettes of whipped cream over the trifle. Dust with cocoa powder.

Caramel and Chocolate Mousse Parfait

2 cups heavy cream
¾ cup granulated sugar
⅓ cup water
½ stick (¼ cup) unsalted butter, softened
1 teaspoon vanilla extract

Chocolate Mousse (page 193)
Whipped cream, for garnish

Yield: 8 servings

- In a small saucepan, bring 1 cup of the cream to a simmer. Remove from the heat and set aside.

- In a small heavy saucepan, dissolve the sugar in the water over low heat. Bring to a boil over medium-high heat, stirring constantly, then let boil without stirring until the syrup turns a deep amber. Remove the pan from the heat and stir in the hot cream (be careful, it will bubble rapidly) and the butter; stir until smooth. Transfer the caramel to a small bowl, cover, and refrigerate until cold, about 1½ hours.

- In a medium bowl, beat the remaining 1 cup cream with the vanilla until soft peaks form. Gently fold in the chilled caramel and refrigerate.

- Set out eight clear, stemmed glasses. Spoon a layer of Chocolate Mousse into each glass, using half of the mousse; smooth the surfaces. Top with layers of caramel mousse in each glass, using half of the mousse; smooth the surfaces. Repeat, spooning in second layers of both the Chocolate Mousse and the caramel mousse.

- Top with rosettes of whipped cream.

Chocolate Crème Brûlée

2 cups heavy cream
3 ounces semisweet chocolate, finely chopped
6 large egg yolks
¼ cup plus 2 tablespoons granulated sugar

2 teaspoons vanilla extract
2 tablespoons dark brown sugar

Yield: 6 servings

● Preheat the oven to 300°F. In a medium saucepan, bring the cream to a simmer. Remove the pan from the heat. Add the chocolate and stir until smooth and melted.

● In a medium bowl, whisk the egg yolks. Beat in ¼ cup of the granulated sugar. Slowly whisk the hot chocolate mixture into the yolks. Whisk in the vanilla. Cool to room temperature.

● Arrange six 6-ounce ramekins or custard cups in a baking pan. Divide the chocolate mixture among the ramekins. Fill the pan with water so it comes halfway up the sides of the cups. Bake for 40 minutes, or until the custard is set. Remove the custards from the water and cool on wire racks. Refrigerate the custards overnight.

● Preheat the broiler. In a small bowl, thoroughly combine the remaining 2 tablespoons granulated sugar with the brown sugar. Toss to break up any clumps in the brown sugar. Sprinkle the sugar mixture evenly over the tops of the custards.

● Broil the custards 2 inches from the heat source for 1 minute, or less, to melt the sugar. Watch the custards carefully so that the sugar melts and lightly caramelizes but does not burn. Let stand for 5 minutes before serving.

For the water bath, choose a baking pan large enough for the ramekins to fit comfortably without touching one another. Pour hot water into the pan to come halfway up the sides of the ramekins.

White Chocolate Bread Pudding

16 ounces white chocolate, coarsely chopped
4 cups light cream or half-and-half
½ cup granulated sugar
8 large eggs, lightly beaten
1 tablespoon vanilla extract
6 tablespoons unsalted butter, softened
10 ounces day-old French bread,
  cut into ¾-inch-thick slices

2 bananas, sliced
2 tablespoons light brown sugar
2 teaspoons cinnamon
Whipped cream and banana slices,
  for garnish

Yield: 12 servings

- Preheat the oven to 350°F. Lightly butter a 9-by-13-inch baking dish.

- Place the chocolate in a medium bowl. In a large heavy saucepan, bring the cream and granulated sugar to a simmer. Pour the hot cream over the chocolate. Let stand, covered, for 5 minutes, then stir until smooth. Beat the eggs and vanilla into the chocolate mixture.

- Butter the bread slices and then cut into cubes. Layer half of the bread into the bottom of the prepared baking dish. Top the bread layer with the banana slices. Top with the remaining bread, then pour in the custard. Press the top of the pudding gently with a spatula to be sure that the bread at the top soaks up some of the custard. Cover the dish with aluminum foil.

- Bake the pudding for 45 minutes, or until the custard is set.

- Meanwhile, in a small bowl, combine the brown sugar and cinnamon.

- When the pudding is set, remove the foil and sprinkle evenly with the cinnamon topping and return to the oven; increase the oven temperature to 450°F and bake for 3 to 4 minutes to brown the top and caramelize the topping.

- Cut into rectangles and serve warm, garnished with whipped cream and banana slices.

White Chocolate Pudding

10 ounces white chocolate, finely chopped
2 tablespoons plus 1 teaspoon cornstarch
2 cups milk
1 teaspoon vanilla extract

Raspberry Sauce (optional; page 197)
Fresh raspberries, for garnish

Yield: 4 servings

- Place the white chocolate in a bowl and set aside.

- In a small bowl, blend the cornstarch with ½ cup of the milk.

- In a small heavy saucepan, bring the remaining 1½ cups milk to a simmer. Whisk in the cornstarch mixture and cook, stirring constantly, until the pudding mixture thickens, about 15 minutes.

- Pour the pudding mixture through a fine-mesh sieve over the chocolate. Let stand for 5 minutes, then add the vanilla and stir until smooth.

- Pour the pudding into four custard cups or dessert bowls, cover tightly, and refrigerate until thoroughly chilled, about 2 hours.

- Serve the puddings with Raspberry Sauce, if desired, and garnish with fresh raspberries.

Chocolate Mousse Cups

2 cups heavy cream
6 ounces semisweet chocolate, finely chopped
¼ cup powdered sugar
1 teaspoon vanilla extract

Chocolate Dessert Cups (page 230)
Candied violets, for garnish (optional)

Yield: 8 to 12 servings

- In a small heavy saucepan, bring ½ cup of the heavy cream to a simmer. Remove from the heat, stir in the chocolate, and cover. Set aside for 5 minutes, then stir until smooth. Transfer the chocolate cream to a large bowl.

- In another large bowl, with an electric mixer, beat the remaining 1½ cups cream with the sugar and vanilla until soft peaks form. Fold one-third of the whipped cream into the chocolate mixture to lighten it. Gently fold in the remaining whipped cream.

- To assemble: Pipe the mousse decoratively into the Chocolate Dessert Cups (or simply spoon the mousse into individual dessert bowls). Garnish with candied violets, if desired.

The Really Easy Chocolate Dessert

7 ounces semisweet chocolate,
    coarsely chopped
1 cup heavy cream
1 large egg, well beaten
2 teaspoons vanilla extract

Sliced bananas, whipped cream, and
    chocolate sprinkles, for garnish

Yield: 4 servings

• In a medium saucepan, melt the chocolate with the cream, stirring constantly. Whisking constantly, stir in the beaten egg and cook, continuing to stir, until bubbles appear on the surface. Remove from the heat.

• Pour the mixture into a blender, add the vanilla, and mix on high speed for 1 minute.

• Pour the chocolate cream into dessert cups or glasses and chill until ready to serve. Serve garnished with banana slices, whipped cream, and chocolate sprinkles.

Pour the chocolate cream from the blender container directly into dessert cups or stemmed glasses.

Chocolate Soufflé with Caramel Crème Anglaise

SOUFFLÉ

½ stick (¼ cup) unsalted butter
3 tablespoons unsweetened cocoa powder
2 tablespoons cornstarch
½ cup milk
6 ounces semisweet chocolate, finely chopped
3 large egg yolks
2 teaspoons vanilla extract
6 large egg whites
½ teaspoon cream of tartar
½ cup granulated sugar

CARAMEL CRÈME ANGLAISE

¾ cup granulated sugar
¼ cup water
1½ cups heavy cream, scalded
1 stick (½ cup) unsalted butter, softened
4 large egg yolks
1 teaspoon vanilla extract
Chocolate Scrolls (page 229) and powdered
  sugar, for garnish

Yield: 6 servings

- Preheat the oven to 350°F. Butter and sugar six 8-ounce soufflé dishes. Place the dishes on a baking sheet.

- Make the soufflé: In a double boiler, melt the butter. Add the cocoa and cornstarch, and stir until smooth. Slowly stir in the milk until smooth. Add the chocolate and remove from the heat for 5 minutes; stir until smooth.

- In a small bowl, stir together the yolks and vanilla. Whisk ½ cup of the chocolate mixture into the yolks to warm them. Whisk the warmed yolks into the chocolate mixture in the double boiler.

- In a medium bowl, beat the egg whites until foamy. Add the cream of tartar and beat until soft peaks form. Slowly add the sugar and beat until stiff, glossy peaks form.

- Transfer the chocolate mixture to a large bowl. Stir one-fourth of the egg whites into the mixture to lighten it. Gently but thoroughly fold in the remaining whites. Transfer the mixture to the soufflé dishes. Place the baking sheet on the bottom rack of the oven and bake for 25 to 30 minutes, or until a toothpick inserted halfway between the edge and the center comes out clean.

- Meanwhile, make the crème anglaise: In a heavy medium saucepan, dissolve the sugar in the water over low heat, stirring constantly. Bring to a boil over medium-high heat, then boil without stirring until the syrup turns a deep amber. While the syrup is boiling, brush down the sides of the pan occasionally to keep crystals from forming. Remove from the heat and stir in the cream (be careful, it will bubble rapidly) and butter; stir to dissolve the caramel.

- In a small bowl, beat the egg yolks. Whisk ½ cup of the hot caramel into the yolks to warm them. Transfer the warmed yolks to the saucepan and stir over low heat until the sauce thickens and heavily coats the back of a spoon, about 5 minutes. Remove from the heat and stir in the vanilla. Strain the sauce through a sieve and keep warm. Garnish the soufflés with Chocolate Scrolls and powdered sugar. Serve with the caramel crème anglaise.

Fallen Soufflé

6 tablespoons unsalted butter, softened
¾ cup granulated sugar
½ cup all-purpose flour
4 ounces semisweet chocolate, finely chopped
½ cup heavy cream
4 large eggs, separated

Pinch of salt
Powdered sugar, for dusting
Vanilla ice cream, for serving

Yield: 8 servings

- Preheat the oven to 350°F. Butter and sugar a 2-quart, 8-inch-diameter soufflé dish.

- In a medium bowl with an electric mixer, cream the butter and ½ cup of the sugar until light and fluffy. Beat in the flour until blended.

- In a double boiler, melt the chocolate with the cream, stirring frequently until smooth. Slowly beat the chocolate cream into the butter-sugar mixture, then return the chocolate mixture to the double boiler. Cook over medium-low heat, stirring constantly, for 7 to 8 minutes, or until thickened. Remove from the heat.

- In a large bowl, lightly beat the egg yolks. Whisk one-fourth of the hot chocolate mixture into the egg yolks to warm them. Return the warmed egg yolk mixture to the saucepan.

- In a medium bowl, beat the egg whites with the salt until foamy. Slowly add the remaining ¼ cup sugar and beat until stiff, glossy peaks form. Stir one-fourth of the egg whites into the chocolate batter to lighten it. Gently and thoroughly fold in the remaining egg whites.

- Spoon the batter into the prepared dish. Set the dish in a deep baking pan and fill the pan with 1 inch of lukewarm water. Bake in the water bath for 1 hour and 10 minutes, or until puffed.

- Remove from the water bath and let stand for 15 minutes, then loosen the edges and invert the soufflé onto a serving plate. Chill until serving time.

- Cut the fallen soufflé into wedges, dust with powdered sugar, and serve with a scoop of vanilla ice cream.

Whisk about one-fourth of the hot chocolate mixture into the beaten egg yolks to warm them.

White Chocolate Soufflé

SOUFFLÉ

8 ounces white chocolate, coarsely chopped
½ cup granulated sugar
⅓ cup milk
4 large egg yolks
1 teaspoon vanilla extract
6 large egg whites
½ teaspoon cream of tartar

RASPBERRY SAUCE

One 12-ounce package unsweetened frozen
  raspberries
¼ cup granulated sugar
1 tablespoon orange juice
Powdered sugar, for dusting

Yield: 6 to 8 servings

- Make the soufflé: In a double boiler, melt the white chocolate over hot, not simmering, water. Set aside to cool slightly.

- Preheat the oven to 350°F. Butter and sugar a ½-quart soufflé dish.

- In a small saucepan, combine the sugar and milk. Cook over medium heat, stirring constantly, until the sugar dissolves, about 3 minutes. Transfer the mixture to a medium bowl. Whisk in the melted white chocolate, egg yolks, and vanilla until well blended.

- In a medium bowl, beat the egg whites and cream of tartar until stiff peaks form. Fold the egg whites into the white chocolate mixture.

- Spoon the mixture into the prepared soufflé dish. With a knife, cut a circle into the top of the soufflé

1 inch in from the edge and about 1 inch deep. Bake the soufflé for 25 to 30 minutes, or until the top is puffed, golden brown, and firm (the inside will still be jiggly).

- Meanwhile, make the sauce: Drain the berries in a fine-mesh sieve set over a bowl; press gently on the berries to remove as much juice as possible. Transfer the juice to a small saucepan and simmer until reduced to about ⅓ cup. Return the reduced juice to the bowl and stir in the sugar and orange juice. With a wooden spoon press the raspberries through the strainer into the bowl. Stir to combine the purée with the juice.

- Remove the soufflé from the oven, dust with powdered sugar, and serve immediately with the raspberry sauce.

Mocha Soufflé

½ cup milk
1¼ cups granulated sugar
6 ounces unsweetened chocolate,
  finely chopped
2 teaspoons instant espresso granules

6 large egg whites
4 large egg yolks
Powdered sugar, for dusting

Yield: 8 servings

- Preheat the oven to 350°F. Butter six 6-ounce soufflé dishes.

- In a medium saucepan, combine the milk and 1 cup of the sugar. Cook, stirring occasionally, over medium-low heat until the sugar dissolves, 5 to 10 minutes. Reduce the heat to low. Add the chocolate and coffee granules, then stir until the mixture is melted and smooth. Set aside to cool to lukewarm.

- In a large bowl, beat the egg whites until foamy. Slowly add the remaining ¼ cup sugar and beat until stiff but not dry peaks form. In a medium bowl, lightly beat the egg yolks.

- Whisk the chocolate mixture into the yolks until well blended. Whisk one-fourth of the egg whites into the chocolate mixture to lighten it. Gently and thoroughly fold in the remaining egg whites.

- Divide the mixture evenly among the prepared soufflé dishes. Bake for 10 to 12 minutes, or until puffed. Remove from the oven, dust with confectioners' sugar, and serve immediately.

With a whisk, beat one-fourth of the egg whites into the chocolate mixture to lighten it (far left). Then, with a spatula, gently but thoroughly fold in the remaining egg whites (near left), taking care not to deflate the soufflé mixture.

Lemony Chocolate-Flecked Soufflés

SOUFFLÉS
1 cup heavy cream
4 teaspoons finely grated lemon peel
½ cup granulated sugar
1 tablespoon cornstarch
3 tablespoons fresh lemon juice
3 large egg yolks
1 tablespoon lemon jam or marmalade
   (optional)
6 egg whites
¼ teaspoon cream of tartar

4 ounces semisweet chocolate,
   coarsely chopped

VANILLA CREAM
2 large egg yolks
½ cup granulated sugar
1 cup heavy cream
½ teaspoon vanilla extract

Yield: 6 servings

- Preheat the oven to 375°F. Butter and sugar six 10-ounce soufflé dishes or custard dishes and place them on a baking sheet.

- Make the soufflés: In a small saucepan, bring the cream and lemon peel to a simmer. Remove from the heat, cover, and let steep for 15 minutes.

- In a small bowl, whisk together ¼ cup of the sugar and the cornstarch. Whisk in the lemon juice and egg yolks until smooth.

- Whisking constantly, add the hot cream to the egg yolk mixture. Strain the lemon cream mixture back into the saucepan and cook, stirring constantly, until thickened; do not boil. Transfer the lemon cream to a large bowl and set aside to cool for 15 minutes. Stir in the lemon jam, if using.

- In a medium bowl with an electric mixer, beat the egg whites until foamy. Add the cream of tartar and beat until soft peaks form. Slowly beat in the remaining ¼ cup sugar and continue beating until

stiff peaks form.

- Fold one-third of the beaten whites into the cooled lemon cream to lighten it. Then fold in the remaining whites along with the chopped chocolate.

- Divide the soufflé mixture among the prepared soufflé dishes. Place the baking sheet in the oven and bake for 18 to 20 minutes, or until puffed and golden brown on top.

- Meanwhile, make the vanilla cream: In a small bowl, whisk the yolks and sugar together.

- In a small saucepan, bring the cream to a simmer. Whisking constantly, beat the hot cream into the yolk mixture. Transfer this custard to the saucepan and cook over low heat, stirring constantly, until the custard coats the back of a spoon. Remove from the heat and stir in the vanilla.

- Strain the vanilla cream into a sauceboat and serve alongside the soufflés.

Chocolate Porcupine Bombe

CHOCOLATE MOUSSE
3 ounces semisweet chocolate
¼ cup light corn syrup
¼ cup plus 2 tablespoons granulated sugar
3 large egg yolks
1 teaspoon vanilla extract
1¼ cups heavy cream

ASSEMBLY
2 quarts chocolate chip ice cream,
  softened slightly

1¾ cups chocolate chip cookie crumbs
2 tablespoons unsalted butter, softened
1 teaspoon unflavored gelatin
4 teaspoons water
2 cups heavy cream
¼ cup granulated sugar
2 teaspoons vanilla extract

Yield: 6 to 8 servings

- Line a 2-quart, 9-inch-diameter stainless steel bowl with foil and place in the freezer while you make the mousse.

- Make the mousse: In a double boiler, melt the chocolate over hot, not simmering, water. Set aside to cool to room temperature.

- In a medium bowl set over a saucepan of simmering water, combine the corn syrup, sugar, and egg yolks. With an electric mixer, beat the egg yolk mixture constantly until it is very thick and pale and warm to the touch. Remove the bowl from the water bath and continue beating until the eggs are cool. Stir in the melted chocolate and vanilla.

- In another medium bowl, beat the cream until soft peaks form. Stir one-fourth of the whipped cream into the chocolate mixture to lighten it, then gently

but thoroughly fold in the remaining whipped cream. Chill the mousse in the freezer for 1 hour.

- Meanwhile, begin to assemble the bombe: Spread the softened ice cream in the chilled foil-lined bowl to a uniform thickness of about 1½ inches, extending up to the rim. Return to the freezer until firm.

- Spoon the chilled mousse into the ice cream-lined bowl and smooth the surface. Return to the freezer for 1 hour.

- Meanwhile, in a food processor or blender, combine the cookie crumbs and butter, then process until finely ground.

- Press the cookie crumbs over the surface of the mousse and return to the freezer while you make the topping.

200

- In a small heatproof measuring cup, combine the gelatin and water and set aside to soften, about 5 minutes. Place the measuring cup in a pan of simmering water and stir occasionally to dissolve the gelatin. Remove the cup and set aside to cool to room temperature.

- In a medium bowl with an electric mixer, beat the cream with the sugar and vanilla until it is just beginning to thicken. Slowly pour in the cooled gelatin mixture, beating constantly. Beat the cream until stiff peaks form, being very careful not to overbeat. Immediately transfer the stabilized whipped cream to a pastry bag fitted with a medium (#5) star tip.

- Remove the bombe from the freezer and invert onto a serving plate. Carefully remove the foil. Pipe rosettes of whipped cream over the surface of the bombe, starting at the base and working to the top. Serve immediately or return the bombe to the freezer until serving time.

Spread the softened ice cream in the foil-lined bowl to a uniform thickness of 1½ inches.

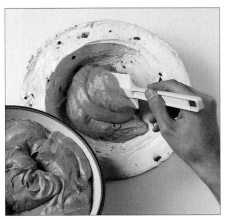

Far left, fill the center of the bombe with the chilled chocolate mousse. Near left, decorate the surface of the unmolded bombe with rosettes of stabilized whipped cream.

Chocolate Caramel Ice Cream

4 large egg yolks
⅛ teaspoon salt
¾ cup granulated sugar
2 tablespoons water
3 cups half-and-half or light cream, at
  room temperature

4 ounces semisweet or bittersweet chocolate,
  finely chopped

Yield: 1½ pints

- In a medium bowl, whisk the yolks and salt until combined.

- In a heavy, medium saucepan, dissolve the sugar in the water over low heat. Bring to a boil over medium-high heat, stirring constantly, then boil without stirring until the syrup turns a deep amber. Remove the pan from the heat and carefully stir in the half-and-half (be careful, the mixture will bubble rapidly). Return to the heat and continue cooking, stirring to dissolve any hardened caramel. Cook until the mixture comes to a gentle boil, 7 to 10 minutes.

- Whisk about half of the hot caramel mixture into the egg yolks to warm them. Return the warmed eggs to the saucepan and continue cooking over low heat, stirring constantly, until the mixture coats the back of a spoon, about 10 minutes. Whisk in the chocolate until smooth.

- Strain the ice cream base into a bowl and let cool to room temperature. Refrigerate until well chilled, at least 4 hours or overnight.

- Transfer the mixture to an ice cream maker and freeze according to the manufacturer's directions. Serve the ice cream soft-frozen, or transfer to an airtight container and freeze until serving time.

Decadent White Chocolate Ice Cream

18 ounces white chocolate, coarsely chopped
2 cups half-and-half or light cream
6 large egg yolks
¾ cup granulated sugar
1½ cups heavy cream, chilled

2 teaspoons vanilla extract
Pieces of cookie, for garnish

Yield: About 5 cups

- In a double boiler, melt 14 ounces of the chocolate over hot, not simmering, water. Set aside to cool slightly.

- In a medium saucepan, bring the half-and-half just to a simmer over medium heat. Remove the pan from the heat.

- In a double boiler, whisk together the egg yolks and sugar until pale. Slowly whisk in the hot half-and-half until well blended. Cook over simmering water, whisking constantly, until thick enough to coat the back of a spoon, about 12 minutes. Remove the double boiler top from the water.

- Add the melted chocolate, stirring until well blended. Stir in the chilled heavy cream and the vanilla. Refrigerate the ice cream mixture until well chilled, at least 4 hours.

- Stir the reserved 4 ounces of chopped white chocolate into the mixture and transfer to an ice cream maker. Freeze according to the manufacturer's directions. Serve the ice cream soft-frozen or transfer to an airtight container and freeze until serving time. Garnish each serving with pieces of cookie, if desired.

Super Hot Fudge Sauce

4 ounces semisweet chocolate,
  coarsely chopped
5 tablespoons unsalted butter
¼ cup unsweetened cocoa powder
¾ cup granulated sugar

¾ cup water
¼ cup light corn syrup
2 teaspoons vanilla extract

Yield: About 1½ cups

● In a heavy medium saucepan, combine the chocolate, butter, cocoa, sugar, water, and corn syrup. Whisk over medium-high heat until the chocolate and butter are melted and the sugar is dissolved. When the sauce just comes to a boil, reduce the heat to low and cook at a low boil for 8 to 10 minutes; the sauce will thicken as it cools. (If the sauce is too thick, thin it with a little water.) Add the vanilla and stir to combine. Store in the refrigerator tightly covered.

Triple Chocolate Suicide

8 ounces white chocolate, finely chopped
8 ounces milk chocolate, finely chopped
6 ounces semisweet chocolate, finely chopped
3 cups heavy cream
2 teaspoons instant coffee granules,
  preferably espresso

Raspberry Sauce (page 197) or Super Hot
  Fudge Sauce (page 204)

Yield: 12 servings

- Line a 6-cup terrine or loaf pan with foil so that the foil extends 2 inches beyond the two short ends.

- Place the white chocolate, milk chocolate, and semisweet chocolate in 3 separate bowls.

- In a medium saucepan, bring the cream to a simmer. Pour 1 cup of the warm cream over the white chocolate, 1 cup of the cream over the milk chocolate, and the remaining 1 cup cream over the semisweet chocolate. Stir each of the mixtures, while the cream is still warm, until melted and smooth.

- Add the instant coffee to the milk chocolate mixture and, with an electric mixer, beat the mocha mixture until it is the consistency of sour cream, 4 to 5 minutes. Spread the mixture in the bottom of the prepared terrine. Freeze until just firm, about 30 minutes.

- Beat the white chocolate mixture until the consistency of sour cream, 4 to 5 minutes. Spread over the mocha layer. Freeze until the white chocolate layer is just firm, about 30 minutes.

- Meanwhile, beat the semisweet mixture until the consistency of sour cream, 4 to 5 minutes. Spoon this mixture over the white chocolate layer and smooth the top. Cover with foil and freeze until firm, 3 hours or overnight.

- Lift up the foil to remove the terrine from the pan. Invert the terrine onto a platter and remove the foil. Cut the terrine into ½- to ¾-inch slices. Serve the terrine with Raspberry Sauce or Super Hot Fudge Sauce. (If using the Super Hot Fudge Sauce, cook the sauce for a shorter amount of time than called for in the recipe to produce a chocolate syrup rather than a thick fudge sauce.)

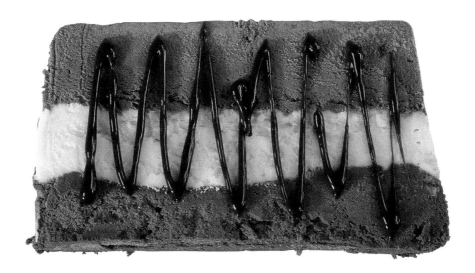

Chocolate Chunk Ice Cream Sandwiches

2½ cups all-purpose flour
½ teaspoon baking soda
¼ teaspoon salt
1 cup granulated sugar
½ cup (packed) light brown sugar
2 sticks (1 cup) unsalted butter
2 large eggs

1 teaspoon vanilla extract
8 ounces semisweet chocolate, cut
 into chunks
2 cups mini semisweet chocolate chips
2 quarts chocolate ice cream, slightly softened

Yield: 16 ice cream sandwiches

- Preheat the oven to 300°F. In a medium bowl, whisk together the flour, baking soda, and salt.

- In a large bowl with an electric mixer, blend the granulated and brown sugars. Add the butter and beat to form a grainy paste. Add the eggs, one at a time, and the vanilla, then beat at medium speed until fully combined. Add the flour mixture and blend at low speed until just combined; do not overmix. Fold in the chocolate chunks.

- For each cookie, drop 2 tablespoons of dough onto an ungreased cookie sheet, leaving about 3 inches space between the cookies. Pat the dough lightly to a ¼-inch thickness.

- Bake for 20 to 22 minutes, or until the cookies are lightly browned around the edges. Cool for 5 minutes on the cookie sheet, then transfer the cookies to a wire rack to cool completely.

- Place the chocolate chips in a shallow bowl or plate. Spread ½ cup of ice cream on each of 16 cookies. Top with a second cookie and press the two halves together to push the ice cream slightly beyond the edges of the cookies. Roll the edges of the ice cream sandwiches in the chocolate chips to coat them and to even out the edges of the sandwich. Wrap each sandwich tightly in plastic wrap and freeze until firm, about 4 hours.

When rolling the ice cream sandwiches in the chocolate chips, press lightly to even out the edges of the ice cream.

Fudgiana Sticks

2 bananas
2 cups coarsely chopped milk chocolate
1 cup finely chopped macadamia nuts

Yield: 4 servings

- Cut the bananas in half crosswise. Insert a popsicle stick into the cut end of each banana half. Wrap each banana popsicle in foil and place in the freezer until frozen.

- In a double boiler, melt the chocolate over hot, not simmering, water. Stir until smooth. Remove from the heat.

- Place the chopped nuts on a sheet of wax paper. Dip the frozen bananas into the melted chocolate and, just as the chocolate is beginning to set but is still slightly soft, roll the bananas in the nuts.

- Serve immediately or rewrap in foil and return to the freezer.

The safest method of melting chocolate is in a double boiler; the modified heat keeps the chocolate from scorching. Just be sure that the chocolate is melted over hot and not simmering water: If the steam released by boiling or simmering water condenses in the chocolate, it will cause the melted chocolate to stiffen or "seize."

Ice Cream Brownie Sandwich

BROWNIES

6 ounces semisweet chocolate,
  coarsely chopped
1 stick (½ cup) unsalted butter
2 cups all-purpose flour
1 teaspoon baking soda
½ teaspoon salt
1½ cups (packed) light brown sugar
4 large eggs
6 ounces mini semisweet chocolate chips

ASSEMBLY AND GLAZE

3 cups ice cream, softened slightly
½ cup heavy cream
6 ounces semisweet chocolate chips
White chocolate hearts, for garnish

Yield: 32 ice cream sandwiches

- Preheat the oven to 350°F. Butter the bottom of an 11-by-17-inch jelly-roll pan. Line the pan with parchment or wax paper and butter the paper.

- Make the brownies: In a double boiler, melt the chocolate and butter over hot, not simmering, water, stirring until melted. Set aside to cool to room temperature.

- In a small bowl, whisk together the flour, baking soda, and salt.

- In a medium bowl, beat the sugar and eggs together until thickened, about 5 minutes. Beat in the melted chocolate mixture. Fold in the flour mixture and the mini chocolate chips. Pour the batter into the prepared pan and smooth the surface. Bake for 15 minutes, or until a cake tester comes out clean. Cool the cake in the pan on a rack for 10 minutes.

- Carefully invert the cake onto a work surface and peel off the parchment paper. With a 2-inch round cookie cutter, cut cookies out from the brownie while it is still slightly warm. Place the brownie rounds in the freezer while you soften up the ice

cream in the refrigerator for 20 minutes.

- Assemble the sandwiches: Cut each brownie round horizontally in half. Spread one half with ¼ inch (about 4 teaspoons) of softened ice cream and top with the other half. As you work, place each finished sandwich in the freezer so it does not melt as you assemble the remaining sandwiches. Freeze the sandwiches until firm.

- Meanwhile, make the glaze: In a small heavy saucepan, scald the cream. Remove from the heat, add the chocolate chips, cover, and let sit for 5 minutes. Stir until smooth. Keep warm and pourable.

- Set the ice cream sandwiches on a wire rack set over a baking sheet. Spoon the warm glaze over the top of the sandwich letting it run down the sides to cover the sandwich completely. Repeat with the remaining sandwiches. Garnish each sandwich with a white chocolate heart, if desired. Return to the freezer to set the glaze and firm the ice cream, about 30 minutes.

Sweetie Pie Cookie Dough Ice Cream

2 ounces unsweetened chocolate
1¾ cups semisweet chocolate chips
1 stick (½ cup) unsalted butter
1 cup granulated sugar
2 teaspoons vanilla extract
2 tablespoons water
1 cup all-purpose flour
½ cup white chocolate chips

¼ cup milk chocolate chips
2 quarts chocolate or vanilla ice cream,
  slightly softened
Fudge Sauce (page 211) and mixed
  chocolate chips, for garnish

Yield: About 3 quarts

- In a double boiler, melt the unsweetened chocolate and ¾ cup of the chocolate chips over hot, not simmering, water. Stir until smooth.

- In a medium bowl, cream the butter and sugar. Add the vanilla and water and beat until smooth. Beat in the melted chocolate. Add the flour, white chocolate chips, milk chocolate chips, and remaining 1 cup semisweet chocolate chips; mix at low speed until the chips are evenly distributed throughout the dough.

- Drop the dough by the teaspoon into the softened ice cream and stir to mix, partially blending the dough into the ice cream. Return to the freezer to firm up before serving.

- Serve the ice cream with Fudge Sauce and a sprinkling of chocolate chips.

Frozen Chocolate Mint Mousse

8 ounces semisweet chocolate, finely chopped
2 large egg whites
2 pinches of cream of tartar
½ cup granulated sugar
¼ cup water
1 cup heavy cream, chilled
3 tablespoons crème de menthe

½ cup semisweet chocolate chips,
  coarsely chopped
Whipped cream and fresh mint,
  for garnish

Yield: 4 to 6 servings

- In a double boiler, melt the chocolate over hot, not simmering, water. Set aside to cool slightly.

- Meanwhile, beat the egg whites with a pinch of cream of tartar until stiff peaks form.

- In a small saucepan, boil the sugar and water with another pinch of cream of tartar until it reaches 234°F to 240°F on a candy thermometer (soft-ball stage), 10 to 12 minutes.

- With the mixer going, carefully pour the hot sugar syrup into the egg whites to make a stiff, glossy meringue. Fold the melted chocolate into the meringue to make chewy lumps.

- In a medium bowl, beat the heavy cream until soft peaks form. Add the crème de menthe and keep beating until stiff peaks form. Fold the chopped chocolate chips into the whipped cream, then fold the whipped cream into the chocolate meringue, leaving streaks of whipped cream. Spoon the mousse into individual dessert bowls or glasses, cover with plastic wrap and freeze until firm, about 2 hours.

- Serve garnished with whipped cream and fresh mint.

Creamy Mocha Ice Cream Shake

FUDGE SAUCE

4 ounces semisweet chocolate,
  coarsely chopped
5 tablespoons unsalted butter
¼ cup unsweetened cocoa powder
¾ cup granulated sugar
¾ cup water
¼ cup light corn syrup
2 teaspoons vanilla extract

SHAKES

½ cup milk
1 teaspoon instant coffee granules
1 teaspoon coffee liqueur
  (optional)
1½ cups vanilla ice cream
Whipped cream and chocolate shavings,
  for garnish

Yield: 2 servings

- Make the fudge sauce: In a heavy medium saucepan, combine the chocolate, butter, cocoa, sugar, water, and corn syrup. Whisk over medium-high heat until the chocolate and butter are melted and the sugar is dissolved. When the sauce just comes to a boil, reduce the heat to low and cook at a low boil for 8 to 10 minutes; the sauce will thicken as it cools. Add the vanilla and stir to combine. Let cool to room temperature, then store in the refrigerator until ready to use. (This fudge sauce recipe makes enough for six ice cream shakes. If you are only making two, refrigerate remaining fudge sauce and keep on hand as a convenient ice cream topping.)

- Make the shakes: In a blender, combine ½ cup of the fudge sauce, the milk, coffee granules, and coffee liqueur (if using). Process until smooth. Add the ice cream and blend until smooth and thick.

- Pour the shakes into tall glasses and garnish with whipped cream rosettes and chocolate shavings.

Super Mud Pie

CRUST
2 cups chocolate wafer crumbs
½ stick (¼ cup) unsalted butter, melted

CARAMEL SAUCE
½ cup granulated sugar
3 tablespoons water
½ cup heavy cream, scalded
½ stick (¼ cup) unsalted butter, softened

ESPRESSO FUDGE SAUCE
4 ounces semisweet chocolate,
  coarsely chopped
¼ cup unsweetened cocoa powder

½ stick (¼ cup) unsalted butter
¾ cup freshly brewed espresso
¾ cup granulated sugar
¼ cup light corn syrup
1 tablespoon coffee liqueur

ASSEMBLY
1 quart vanilla ice cream, softened
½ cup coarsely chopped toasted
  macadamia nuts

Yield: 8 to 10 servings

- Make the crust: Combine the wafer crumbs and melted butter. Press the crumb-and-butter mixture into the bottom and partially up the sides of a 9-inch springform pan.

- Make the caramel sauce: In a small heavy saucepan, dissolve the sugar in the water over low heat, stirring constantly. Bring to a boil over medium-high heat, then let boil without stirring until the syrup turns a light amber. While the syrup is boiling, brush down the sides of the pan from time to time to prevent crystals from forming. Remove the pan from the heat and stir in the hot cream (be careful, it will bubble rapidly). Continue stirring, over low heat if necessary, until all of the caramel is dissolved into the cream. Stir in the butter and set aside to cool slightly. Pour the warm caramel sauce over the crust and freeze the crust until firm, about 30 minutes.

- Make the espresso fudge sauce: In a medium saucepan, combine the chopped chocolate, cocoa,

butter, and espresso. Stir over low heat until smooth. Add the sugar and corn syrup, increase the heat to medium, and stir until the sugar dissolves. Increase the heat until the sauce reaches a low boil. Cook without stirring until the sauce thickens, 12 to 15 minutes. Remove from the heat and stir in the coffee liqueur.

- Cool the sauce to room temperature, then pour 1 cup of the sauce over the caramel layer and return the crust to the freezer. Set the remaining sauce aside and keep just warm enough so it remains pourable.

- Assemble the pie: Spread the softened ice cream over the caramel layer and return to the freezer to firm, about 1 hour. Pour the remaining fudge sauce over the ice cream layer, top with the macadamia nuts, and freeze until firm, about 2 hours.

- Serve: Wrap a hot, wet towel around the springform for 2 minutes to loosen, then remove the sides of the pan.

Mocha Parfait

4 ounces semisweet chocolate,
  coarsely chopped
8 large egg yolks
⅓ cup light corn syrup
⅓ cup granulated sugar

1 tablespoon instant coffee granules
  dissolved in 1 tablespoon coffee liqueur
2 cups heavy cream
Chocolate stick candy, for garnish

Yield: 8 servings

● In a double boiler, melt the chocolate over hot, not simmering, water. Set aside to cool to room temperature.

● In a medium bowl set over a saucepan of simmering water, combine the egg yolks, corn syrup, and sugar. With an electric mixer, beat the egg-yolk mixture constantly until it is very thick and pale and warm to the touch. Remove the bowl from the water bath and continue beating until the eggs are cool.

● Transfer one-third of the egg mixture to a small bowl and stir in the dissolved coffee.

● Mix the melted chocolate into the egg mixture remaining in the medium bowl.

● In another medium bowl, beat the cream until soft peaks form. With a whisk, beat about ½ cup of the whipped cream into the chocolate mixture to lighten it. Then gently but thoroughly fold in two-thirds of the remaining whipped cream. With a whisk, beat in ⅓ cup whipped cream into the coffee mixture to lighten it, then gently but thoroughly fold in the remaining whipped cream.

● Spoon half of the chocolate parfait mixture into eight 1-cup parfait glasses. Place in the freezer for 10 minutes to firm (keep the remaining parfait mixtures in the refrigerator).

● Layer all of the coffee mixture into the parfait glasses and return the parfaits to the freezer to firm. Top the parfaits with the remaining chocolate mixture and freeze until completely firm, about 2 hours.

● Serve the parfait with chocolate stick candy.

The Ultimate Ice Cream Pie

COOKIE CRUMB CRUST
1¼ cups chocolate-chip cookie crumbs

FUDGE SAUCE
2 ounces semisweet chocolate, chopped
2½ tablespoons unsalted butter
¼ cup plus 2 tablespoons granulated sugar
2 tablespoons unsweetened cocoa powder
2 tablespoons corn syrup
¼ cup plus 2 tablespoons water
1 teaspoon vanilla extract

CARAMEL SAUCE
½ cup granulated sugar
2 tablespoons water
¼ cup cream, scalded
2 tablespoons unsalted butter, softened

FILLING
1 cup mini marshmallows
1 cup semisweet chocolate chips
3 cups vanilla ice cream, softened in the
  refrigerator

Yield: One 9-inch pie

- Preheat the oven to 325°F.

- Make the crust: Press the cookie crumbs into the bottom and up the sides of a 9-inch pie plate. Bake for 10 minutes. Cool the crust to room temperature.

- Prepare the fudge sauce: In a small saucepan, melt the chocolate and butter over low heat; stir until smooth. Add the sugar, cocoa, corn syrup, and water and cook until the sugar dissolves. Bring the mixture to a boil and cook at a low boil, without stirring, until the sauce is thick and smooth, about 15 minutes. Remove from the heat and stir in the vanilla. Set aside to cool to lukewarm.

- Make the caramel sauce: In a heavy medium saucepan, dissolve the sugar in the water over low heat, stirring constantly. Bring to a boil over medium-high heat, then let boil, without stirring, until the syrup turns a light amber. While the syrup is boiling, brush down the sides of the pan from time to time with a wet pastry brush to prevent crystals from forming. Remove the pan from the heat and stir in the hot cream (it will bubble rapidly). Stir in the butter and continue stirring the sauce until smooth. Cool the sauce to lukewarm.

- Assemble: Pour the fudge sauce into the pie crust. Chill in the freezer until the sauce is set, about 15 minutes. In a medium bowl, stir the marshmallows and chocolate chips into the softened ice cream. Spread the ice cream mixture over the fudge layer and smooth the top. Place in the freezer until set, about 30 minutes.

- Dip a fork into the caramel sauce and drizzle it in a crisscross pattern over the top of the pie. Return to the freezer for 1 hour to set. Cut the pie into wedges with a sharp knife and serve immediately.

Candy

Coffee Toffee Chocolate Crunch

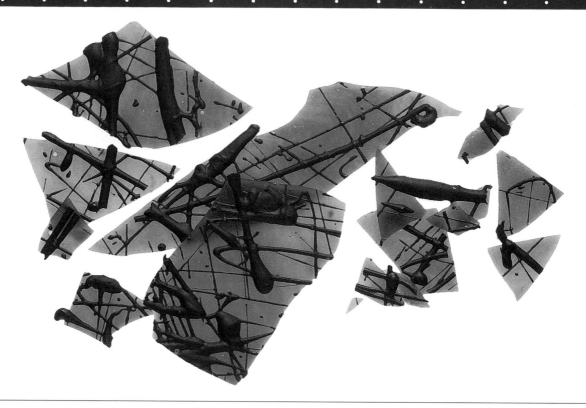

6 tablespoons salted butter
1 cup granulated sugar
¼ cup water

2 teaspoons coffee liqueur
¼ teaspoon baking soda
½ cup (3 ounces) semisweet chocolate chips

• Lightly grease a 9-by-13-inch glass baking dish.

• In a heavy 2-quart saucepan, combine butter, sugar and water. Heat over medium temperature, stirring with a wooden spoon until sugar dissolves. Cover pan for 2 minutes to wash down any sugar crystals.

• Uncover pan and increase heat to high. Without stirring, continue cooking until mixture begins to turn golden brown.

• Quickly remove from heat; stir in coffee liqueur and baking soda. Pour immediately into prepared baking dish. Spread thin with a wooden spoon. Cool to room temperature.

• In a small saucepan, melt chocolate chips, stirring constantly until smooth. Then, dip a fork into the chocolate and drizzle lattice patterns over the toffee candy. Let stand until chocolate is set. Break toffee into irregular-size pieces. Store in an airtight container.

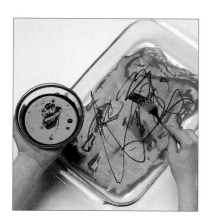

To decorate the cooled toffee, dip a fork into melted chocolate. Let the chocolate drizzle off the tines onto the candy in interesting swirls and lattice patterns. Allow chocolate to set before breaking the candy into bite-size pieces.

Macadamia Nut Brittle

1½ cups (9 ounces) whole macadamia nuts
6 tablespoons salted butter
1 cup granulated sugar
¼ cup water

¼ teaspoon baking soda
1 teaspoon vanilla extract

Yield: About 1 pound of brittle

- Lightly grease a 9-by-13-inch glass baking dish. Equally distribute macadamia nuts over bottom of dish. Set aside.

- In a heavy 2-quart saucepan, combine butter, sugar and water. Place over medium heat and stir with a wooden spoon until sugar dissolves. Let pan stand covered for 2 minutes.

- Uncover pan and increase heat to high. Continue cooking without stirring until mixture begins to turn golden brown. Quickly remove from heat; stir in baking soda and vanilla extract. Pour immediate-ly over macadamia nuts in prepared baking dish. Spread with a wooden spoon.

- Cool to room temperature. Break into irregular-size pieces. Store in an airtight container.

Heat the butter-sugar combination over high heat until it turns a rich, golden brown, as shown at left. Immediately pour the liquid over the macadamia nuts. Use a wooden spoon to distribute the nuts evenly around the pan (right). Allow the brittle to cool before breaking into bite-size pieces.

Mocha Truffles

TRUFFLES

9 ounces semisweet chocolate, finely chopped
¾ cup heavy cream
½ stick (¼ cup) unsalted butter
2 tablespoons instant espresso granules
  blended with 2 tablespoons coffee liqueur

COATING

8 ounces semisweet chocolate
2 teaspoons vegetable oil

Yield: About 2½ dozen

- Make the truffles: Place the chopped chocolate in a medium bowl. In a heavy, medium saucepan, bring the cream and butter to a simmer. Pour the hot cream mixture over the chopped chocolate. Stir the coffee mixture into the chocolate cream. Let stand for 5 minutes, then stir until smooth. Cool to room temperature, then refrigerate until firm enough to form into balls, about 2 hours.

- Roll the truffle mixture into tablespoon-size balls and place on a wax paper-lined cookie sheet. Return to the refrigerator until well chilled and firm.

- Prepare the coating: In a double boiler, melt the chocolate over hot, not simmering, water. Stir until smooth. Remove from the heat and stir in the oil. Let cool to lukewarm.

- Holding a truffle with the first two fingers of one hand, submerge the truffle in the coating. Allow the excess chocolate to drip off, then return to the wax paper. Refrigerate until firm. Store chilled. Let the truffles sit at room temperature for 15 to 20 minutes before serving.

Near right, using about 1 tablespoon of truffle mixture, form into a ball. Far right, holding a well-chilled truffle with the first two fingers of one hand, dip the truffle in the coating chocolate.

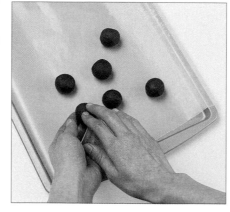

White Chocolate Pralines

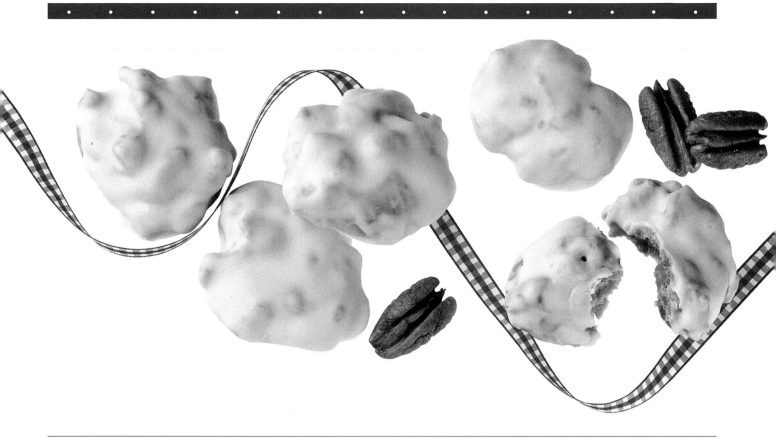

1½ cups granulated sugar
1 cup (packed) light brown sugar
1 cup light cream or half-and-half
2 tablespoons light corn syrup
Pinch of salt
6 tablespoons unsalted butter

1 tablespoon vanilla extract
1½ cups coarsely chopped pecans, toasted
16 ounces white chocolate, finely chopped
1 teaspoon vegetable oil

Yield: About 4 dozen

- Line a cookie sheet with parchment paper or buttered wax paper.

- In a heavy medium saucepan, combine the granulated and brown sugars, the cream, corn syrup, and salt. Stir over medium-low heat until the sugars are dissolved, about 5 minutes. Increase the heat to high and cook, stirring, until the mixture reaches 238° on a candy thermometer.

- Remove the pan from the heat. Add the butter, vanilla, and pecans and beat vigorously until the mixture thickens, 10 to 12 minutes.

- Working quickly, drop the mixture by teaspoon onto the prepared cookie sheet. If the mixture begins to harden, place the pan over low heat to soften it. Cool the pralines (do not refrigerate) until set, about 1 hour.

- Line a second cookie sheet with aluminum foil. In a double boiler, melt the white chocolate with the oil over hot, not simmering, water. Remove the pan from the heat. Dip each candy into the chocolate to coat. Transfer to the cookie sheet and let stand until the chocolate is set, about 30 minutes.

White Fudge with Almonds

1 cup slivered almonds
¾ cup granulated sugar
⅔ cup evaporated milk
½ cup marshmallow creme
2 tablespoons unsalted butter

¼ teaspoon salt
10 ounces white chocolate, finely chopped
¼ teaspoon almond extract

Yield: About 1½ pounds

- Preheat the oven to 350°F. Spread the almonds on a baking sheet and toast in the oven for 10 minutes or until golden. Cool the almonds slightly, then finely chop. Set aside..

- Line an 8-by-8-inch baking pan with foil so that the foil extends 2 inches beyond the pan on two opposite sides.

- In a heavy medium saucepan, combine the sugar, evaporated milk, marshmallow creme, butter and salt. Bring to a boil over medium heat, stirring constantly, until the sugar and marshmallow creme dissolve, about 3 minutes.

- Reduce the heat to low, cover, and simmer for 1 minute; do not stir. Uncover the pan and cook for 5 minutes, stirring frequently. Remove the pan from the heat and add the white chocolate; stir until melted and smooth. Stir in the nuts and almond extract.

- Scrape the fudge into the prepared pan and smooth the top. Chill for 1 hour, or until firm. Remove the fudge from the pan by lifting up the edges of the foil. Cut the fudge into small squares.

Chocolate Rock

6 ounces semisweet chocolate, finely chopped
6 ounces milk chocolate, finely chopped
1 tablespoon vegetable oil
1 cup pecan halves and pieces, toasted

6 ounces white chocolate, coarsely chopped

Yield: About 1¼ pounds

- Line a cookie sheet with aluminum foil.
- In a double boiler, melt the semisweet and milk chocolates with the oil over hot, not simmering, water, stirring constantly until the chocolate is melted and smooth.
- Remove the top part of the double boiler and let the chocolate cool to tepid. (The chocolate may thicken slightly as it cools.)
- Stir the pecans and chopped white chocolate into the cooled melted chocolate and pour the mixture out onto the prepared cookie sheet. Spread to the desired thickness. Refrigerate for 20 to 30 minutes, or until set.
- Slide a metal spatula under the chocolate to loosen from the foil. Break into uneven pieces.

Nutty Milk Chocolate Fudge

1½ sticks (¾ cup) unsalted butter
⅓ cup evaporated milk
¼ cup granulated sugar
6 ounces milk chocolate, finely chopped
6 ounces semisweet chocolate, finely chopped
1 cup marshmallow creme

1 cup peanut butter chips
½ cup unsalted, roasted peanuts,
  coarsely chopped

Yield: About 2 pounds

- Line an 8-by-8-inch baking pan with foil. Lightly butter the foil.

- In a heavy medium saucepan, combine the butter, evaporated milk, and sugar. Bring the mixture to a boil, stirring constantly to dissolve the sugar. Reduce the heat and boil gently, without stirring, for 5 minutes.

- Remove from the heat and stir in the milk chocolate, semisweet chocolate, and marshmallow creme; whisk until smooth. Set aside to cool to lukewarm.

- Stir in the peanut butter chips and peanuts. Pour the mixture into the prepared pan and refrigerate until set, 3 to 4 hours. Cut the fudge into squares.

White Chocolate Pecan Sheets

1 pound white chocolate, finely chopped
1 tablespoon unsalted butter
1 tablespoon vegetable oil

1 cup coarsely chopped toasted pecans
  or pistachios

Yield: About 1¼ pounds

- Line a cookie sheet with aluminum foil.

- In a double boiler, melt the chocolate with the butter and oil over hot, not simmering, water, stirring constantly until the chocolate is melted and smooth.

- Remove the top part of the double boiler and stir the nuts into the melted chocolate. Pour the chocolate mixture out onto the prepared cookie sheet. Spread randomly to the desired thickness. Refrigerate for 20 to 30 minutes, or until set.

- Slide a metal spatula under the chocolate to loosen from the foil. Break into uneven pieces. Store in an airtight container in the refrigerator.

Spread the white chocolate mixture to an uneven thickness over the foil-lined cookie sheet.

Clusters for Kids

COATING
8 ounces milk chocolate, finely chopped
1 tablespoon plus 1 teaspoon vegetable oil

MIX-INS (1⅓ CUPS TOTAL)
Chopped nuts
Raisins

Mini marshmallows
Cereals (especially small, crunchy shapes)
White chocolate or peanut butter chips

Yield: About 16 pieces

- Line a cookie sheet with aluminum foil.

- Make the coating: In a double boiler, melt the chocolate with the oil over hot, not simmering, water, stirring constantly until the chocolate is melted and smooth. Set aside to cool to tepid.

- Prepare the mix-ins: You will need a total of 1⅓ cups of mix-ins. You can use all one ingredient, a combination of several ingredients, or up to 4 different combinations.

- If you are using only one type of mix-in, you can leave the chocolate in the double boiler. If you are trying several different combinations, divide the chocolate mixture among several bowls. Stir the mix-ins into the chocolate, then drop clusters by the heaping tablespoon onto the prepared cookie sheet.

- Refrigerate for about 20 minutes to set the chocolate.

Chocolate-Dipped Fruit

CHOCOLATE COATING
4 ounces semisweet chocolate, finely chopped
2 teaspoons vegetable oil
6 ounces white chocolate, finely chopped

FRUIT
2 pints strawberries with stems, or
3 cups fresh pineapple wedges, or

36 dried apricot or pear halves, or
36 slices of kiwi fruit, or a mixture of fruits
Finely chopped almonds or pistachios,
  for garnish

Yield: 4 to 8 servings

- Line a cookie sheet with foil.

- Prepare the chocolate coating: In a small heatproof bowl set over hot, not simmering, water, melt the semisweet chocolate with 1 teaspoon of the oil. In another small heatproof bowl set over hot, not simmering, water, melt the white chocolate with the remaining 1 teaspoon oil. Leave both bowls over the hot water.

- Pick up one piece of fruit at a time and dip it into the melted dark or white chocolate, coating about half of each piece of fruit. If desired, drizzle the dipped portion with a contrasting color of chocolate and sprinkle with some chopped nuts. Place the fruit on the foil-lined cookie sheet. Work quickly to coat the remaining fruit.

- Refrigerate for 5 minutes or until the chocolate is set. Keep in a cool place until ready to serve. (Fresh fruit should not be held for more than 4 hours before serving.)

Chocolate Crunch

6 ounces semisweet chocolate, finely chopped
6 ounces milk chocolate, finely chopped
1 tablespoon unsalted butter
1 tablespoon vegetable oil
1 cup chopped toasted almonds or
  macadamia nuts

1 cup crisp rice cereal
6 ounces white chocolate, coarsely chopped

Yield: About 1¼ pounds

- Line a cookie sheet with aluminum foil.

- In a double boiler, melt the semisweet and milk chocolates with the butter and oil over hot, not simmering, water, stirring constantly until the chocolate is melted and smooth.

- Remove the top part of the double boiler and let the chocolate cool to tepid. (The chocolate may thicken slightly as it cools.)

- Stir the nuts, cereal, and white chocolate pieces into the cooled melted chocolate and pour the mixture out onto the prepared cookie sheet. Spread to the desired thickness. Refrigerate for 20 to 30 minutes, or until set.

- Slide a metal spatula under the chocolate to loosen from the foil. Break into uneven pieces.

Chocolate Peanut Butter Pieces

18 ounces milk chocolate, finely chopped
    (about 3 cups)
½ cup creamy peanut butter
5 tablespoons powdered sugar, sifted

1 cup salted peanuts, whole and halves

Yield: About 2 pounds

- Line a 9-by-13-inch pan with foil.

- In a double boiler, melt the chocolate over hot, not simmering, water. Stir until smooth.

- Place the peanut butter in a small bowl. Gradually beat in the sugar.

- Add the peanut butter mixture to the chocolate and stir until blended. Set aside to cool slightly.

- Stir in ¾ cup of the peanuts and spread the mixture in the foil-lined pan. Smooth the top, then sprinkle the remaining ¼ cup peanuts over the top, pressing lightly into the candy. Chill until firm, then cut into pieces.

Use a wooden spoon to stir the peanut butter mixture into the melted chocolate.

227

E.G. Fudge

2 sticks (1 cup) unsalted butter
3 cups granulated sugar
½ cup unsweetened cocoa powder
Pinch of salt
3 tablespoons light corn syrup
1 cup condensed milk

½ cup water
1 teaspoon vanilla extract
1 cup coarsely chopped walnuts
2½ cups miniature marshmallows

Yield: About 1½ pounds

- Butter an 8-by-8-inch pan or 9-inch-diameter plate. Set aside the butter in a medium bowl.

- In a large heavy saucepan, whisk together the sugar, cocoa, and salt. Add the corn syrup, condensed milk, and water, then stir with a wooden spoon until thoroughly combined. Cook over low-to-medium heat, stirring constantly, until the mixture comes to a full rolling boil. Boil, without stirring, until the mixture measures 236°F (soft-ball stage) on a candy thermometer. To test for doneness, drop a teaspoon of the mixture in a bowl of iced water and form it into a ball with your fingers. If the ball holds its shape under water but immediately loses shape and flattens between your fingers out of the water, the mixture is ready; otherwise cook a little longer.

- Remove from the heat and pour the chocolate mixture over the butter; do not stir. Let the mixture cool to lukewarm; you should be able to comfortably touch the sides of the bowl with your hands.

- Beat at low speed with an electric mixer to incorporate the butter, then continue beating until the shine begins to come off the mixture (at this point you should be able to comfortably dip your finger in the mixture). Add the vanilla and beat for another 15 minutes or so, until the fudge starts to thicken and falls slowly from the beaters. Stir in the walnuts and marshmallows, then immediately spread the fudge in the prepared pan.

- Let the fudge sit at room temperature until firm enough to cut, about 1 hour.

Chocolate Scrolls & Cut-Outs

For Chocolate Scrolls:
Use a metal spatula to spread melted chocolate on a cookie sheet or a smooth work surface. Let the chocolate stand at room temperature until firmed up but still pliable. Use a wide spatula to scrape the chocolate into a roll. For a looser scroll, scrape up a shorter length of chocolate so that it does not completely close.

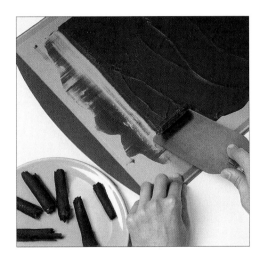

For Chocolate Cut-Outs:
Spread melted chocolate on a sheet of parchment paper or wax paper with a metal spatula. Let the chocolate stand at room temperature until firmed up but still pliable. Use small cookie cutters to cut out a variety of shapes. For more delicate shapes, use extra-small cutters often sold as truffle cutters or aspic cutters.

Chocolate Leaves & Dessert Cups

For Chocolate Dessert Cups:
With a small pastry brush, coat
the insides of paper muffin-cup
liners with melted chocolate.
Chill the cups to set the chocolate
and then brush on a second coat.
If desired, for a sturdier cup,
add a third coat. When the final
coating is set, carefully peel
off the paper.

For Chocolate Leaves:
With a small pastry brush,
paint the underside (vein side) of
a nontoxic leaf—the leaves
shown here are lemon leaves—
with melted chocolate; do not
paint all the way to the edge of
the leaf. Place the coated leaves
in the refrigerator to set the
chocolate, then very carefully
peel the leaf away.

Index

Time-Life Books is a division of
TIME LIFE INC.

Time-Life Custom Publishing

Vice President and Publisher: Terry Newell
Associate Publisher: Teresa Hartnett
Project Manager: Christopher M. Register
Vice President of Sales and Marketing: Neil Levin
Director of Special Sales: Liz Ziehl
Managing Editor: Donia Ann Steele
Production Manager: Carolyn Clark
Quality Assurance Manager: James D. King

Mrs. Fields Best Ever Cookie Book

Editor: Patricia Daniels
Design: REDRUTH, Robin Bray proprietor
Photography: Renée Comet, Lisa Koenig
Indexing: Rose Grant

First printing. Printed in U.S.A.

Time-Life is a trademark of Time Warner Inc. U.S.A.

ISBN: 0-7835-5266-1

Books produced by Time-Life Custom Publishing are
available at special bulk discount for promotional and
premium use. Custom adaptations can also be created
to meet your specific marketing goals.
Call 1-800-323-5255